ADVANCE PRAISE FOR

YOU ARE A F*CKING AWESOME MOM

"I can't think of anyone better suited to write about new motherhood than Leslie Bruce. She's refreshingly honest, ridiculously well researched, nonjudgmental, and always hilarious. And as a parent, I can tell you that sometimes you really need to laugh . . . so that you don't cry." —LAUREN CONRAD

"For those of us who were shocked to discover that modern motherhood is a den of insanity, Leslie Bruce is a lifeline."

—JILL SMOKLER, *New York Times* best-selling author and creator of Scary Mommy

"Finally, a mom who doesn't claim motherhood is all unicorns pooping glittery rainbows. Moms *need* this book."

—KAREN ALPERT, *New York Times* best-selling author of *I Heart My Little A-Holes*

"Leslie Anne Bruce is the mom friend I never knew I needed. With a rare combination of generous spirit and cutting humor, she strips away the clichés of motherhood and teaches us how to survive the raw, real thing."

—LYDIA FITZPATRICK, author of *Lights All Night Long*

"Leslie Bruce's central thesis is one that many women in today's 'have it all' world will feel like a punch to the gut. Fortunately, Bruce also happens to be f*cking hilarious, which makes her book not only an important read, but also a phenomenally fun one."

—JORDAN REID, author of *The Big Fat Activity Book for Pregnant People*

"Honesty—what a fabulous and rare thing that is today. You'll find it in abundance in Leslie Bruce's raw, real, laugh-out-loud account of what becoming a mother is really all about. This book is the stuff you don't see on Instagram. This is a must-read for any new mother."

—RAEGAN MOYA-JONES, author of *What It Takes: How I Built a $100 Million Business Against the Odds* and founder of aden + anais

"Both laugh-out-loud hilarious and surprisingly heartfelt, Leslie Bruce is the no-BS, tell-it-like-it-is online BFF every mom needs while navigating those treacherous early parenting years. Whether it's chronicling what mothers think (but dare not say) or sharing warts-and-all #momfail peeks at the reality of life with a toddler on her addictive Instagram feed, Leslie Bruce's razor-sharp wit and sorely needed honesty are always bright spots in my day."

—NADINE COURTNEY, author of *Romancing the Throne* and *All-American Muslim Girl*

"Leslie is truthful, funny, and transparent without being over the top. Her stories are raw without being negative. We can adore our babies and motherhood, and still have bad days. Leslie encourages women to be open and I find it very empowering!"

—HANNAH TAYLOR, cofounder of The Little Market

YOU ARE A F*CKING AWESOME MOM

YOU ARE A F*CKING AWESOME MOM

So Embrace the Chaos, Get Over the Guilt, and Be True to You

LESLIE BRUCE

SEAL PRESS

Seal Press
Hachette Book Group
1290 Avenue of the Americas, New York, NY 10104
www.sealpress.com
@sealpress

Printed in the United States of America
First Edition: September 2019
Published by Seal Press, an imprint of Perseus Books, LLC, a subsidiary of Hachette Book Group, Inc. The Seal Press name and logo is a trademark of the Hachette Book Group.

Print book interior design by Linda Mark

Library of Congress Cataloging-in-Publication Data
Names: Bruce, Leslie, author.
Title: You are a f*cking awesome mom: so embrace the chaos, lose the guilt, and stay true to you / Leslie Bruce.
Other titles: You are a fucking awesome mom
Description: Berkeley, California: Seal Press, [2019]
Identifiers: LCCN 2018060881| ISBN 9781580058902 (pbk.) | ISBN 9781580058919 (ebook)
Subjects: LCSH: Motherhood. | Motherhood—Humor.
Classification: LCC HQ759 .B75949 2019 | DDC 306.874/3—dc23
LC record available at https://lccn.loc.gov/2018060881

ISBNs: 978-1-58005-890-2 (paperback), 978-1-58005-891-9 (ebook)

LSC-C

10 9 8 7 6 5 4 3 2 1

For my mom,
You are so fucking awesome.
I love you fiercely and I dedicate this book to you.

Now, can you please stop telling people,
"Having one kid is great; having two is horrible."
Everyone knows I was number two, Sandra.

CONTENTS

CONTENTS

Dear Mama,

I want to tell you something you need to know right now: You're a rock star.

Sure, that sounds like a lame saying you'd see on a coffee mug in the "girl boss" aisle at Target, but I mean it . . . you're a badass mama. You're responsible for creating human life. Think about that! That's some superhuman stuff right there. You grew a baby and, most likely, that baby has ears. And who made those ears? You did . . . inside your body! Your baby has ears because of you. Know that, girl.

As mamas, we all have a tendency to get down on ourselves when we have bad days, and, chances are, you've had plenty of them. We beat ourselves up when we don't feel like we're "crushing motherhood." So, whatever feelings of guilt or shame you have—whether it's because you chose not to breastfeed or because you had to go back to work or simply because you're not loving every second of mom life—LET IT GO!

You're using whatever free time you have to read a book on motherhood to be the best mama you can be, so you're already doing an incredible job. If you're like me, then you ventured into motherhood with beautiful ideas of what it would look like, but soon after the newborn glow began to wear off, your daunting new reality started to sink in.

Things aren't always going to go according to plan. There will be days when you feel like you just can't handle it all, and maybe you can't, but that doesn't make you a bad mom . . . it makes you normal. Remind yourself that every day you wake up with the goal of doing your very best for your baby, your family, and yourself, and that is good enough! I spoke to an early childcare therapist about the idea of "good enough" parenting; she said that the goal isn't to be the perfect parent but to be a "good enough" parent, which requires us to do our best at least 50 percent of the time. Anything beyond that is just icing on the cake. I, for one, really like those odds, and I sure wish someone had shared them with me before I became a mom. But what is our responsibility to other women as they become mothers?

A few months after Tallulah was born, my good friend Julie came to visit us. I had just emerged from the haze of the fourth trimester and was finally fit for company (both mentally and physically). We sat around the kitchen table while Tallulah napped, and Julie confided in me that she and her husband were planning to start their own family.

"I know you won't sugarcoat it, Leslie," she started, wide-eyed with excitement, but almost bracing herself. "Just tell me . . . how hard is it?"

I laughed. "Which part?"

"All of it . . ." she said, twirling her hand casually in the air. "How hard is it being a mom?"

If poor Julie would have visited just a few weeks earlier, I would have excused myself to the bathroom to begin frantically searching for leftover birth control pills to crush and sprinkle in her coffee.

Fortunately for her, I was currently of more sound mind.

I thought for a minute about how to answer her seemingly innocent question. How could I be honest with my friend without terrifying her? I knew I had the very undeserved power to shape her perspective on a monumental life event, and I wanted to proceed with caution.

Should I tell her how it feels to have your nipples sucked raw every two hours by a tiny human? Or should I focus on the overwhelming love I feel when my daughter wraps her small hands around my finger? Because it's both. It's a roller-coaster ride punctuated by bursts of complete joy, energy, and overwhelming gratitude as well as exhaustion, sadness, and irrational fits of mania.

It is the best of times and the worst of times.

My lovely friend looked at me from across the table, eager for me to lay down the #momlife gauntlet, as she believed only I could do. And I could. I was certain that my stories could have kept Julie chaste for the foreseeable future.

In my heart, I knew that my friend was gonna be totally screwed. She was a fierce, well-traveled, and incredibly independent woman who had built a hugely successful career as an executive at an athletic wear company.

Though I was certain that my loving, kind, and compassionate friend would be the most amazing mother, I also knew that making the transition from "Boss Lady" to "New Mama" was going to rock her world in unimaginable ways. So, should I tell her she was about to embark on the hardest journey of her life, which nothing could prepare her for, that also included a complete and total identity crisis? That she would spend some days wondering why she ever thought having a baby was a good idea, and then see her child's sweet face only to immediately feel a nausea-inducing sense of guilt for ever wishing to get back her life before motherhood?

"Jules," I finally said. "You're not asking the right question."

"What do you mean?"

"When you're running a marathon, do you focus on the race or the feeling at the finish line?" I paused, being someone who has never run a marathon. "Don't ask about the journey, ask about the reward." (Which is literally the opposite sentiment of every single motivational poster or meme, but . . . whatever.)

"Okay," she replied. "So, what am I asking you?"

"Is it worth it," I said.

She rolled her eyes before deciding to play along: "Well . . ."

"Yes," I said, without hesitation. "Every fucking minute of every fucking day. She's worth all of it and I'd do it again in a heartbeat."

So, to all you new—and new-ish—mamas out there, I'm not going to tell you the best way to take care of your child, because only you know what's best. I may offer some tips or suggestions, but this isn't a baby book. This is a mama book. This is a book for any woman who is still trying to wrap her head around this incredible, insane, all-consuming transition while desperately clinging to any lasting shreds of grace. This is for any new mama or even semi-new mama who feels like she got railroaded by baby and may be struggling with figuring out her new place in life. Most importantly, this book is for any woman who wants to be the best person she can be not only for her baby but also for herself.

When I decided to write this book, I was just coming out of the first year of life with my daughter, Tallulah. My struggle was so real that I wanted to scream it from the rooftops so other moms wouldn't feel as isolated or devalued when their own experience wasn't all puppies and rainbows. I even created Unpacified, a website and media platform dedicated to helping mamas navigate this transition. It turns out that pitching and selling a book can be a lengthy process, during which time I got myself knocked up again. Although this story is largely about my journey with my daughter, I wrote much of what you're about to read while nine months pregnant and during the very early days with my son, Roman. So, if some of what you're about to read feels super fresh, it's because it was . . . it really was. Having your first baby will knock you on your ass, but don't underestimate the juggle of going from one to two.

I'm not going to pretend that stumbling into motherhood is this wholly magical journey or tell you that every single struggle gets wrapped up in a pretty red bow. There are going to be beautiful, picture-perfect, freeze-this-moment-in-time days, but there are also going to be days when you want to crawl out of your skin. And that's okay. I need you to remember that you are entitled to your feelings . . . whatever they are. You're an intelligent, strong woman who is capable of experiencing two conflicting emotions. Motherhood isn't this one-dimensional thing. It's layered as fuck.

But I am going to keep reminding you that you're a warrior. You have gone to battle for your baby, and you deserve respect, adoration, and compassion. You're that child's hero, and even heroes have hard days.

Most of all, I want you to know this: You're not alone.

xo,

Leslie

1

EVERYONE LIED

"It's the hardest, most rewarding thing I've ever done."

After my daughter was born, I was often confronted with the question: "How's new mom life treating you?" For years, I had heard women utter some version of the same "hard but rewarding" sentiment, as if to underscore that the joy far outweighs the challenges. It's a phrase that gives weight and credit to the mothers who came before while also reminding people that nothing could possibly hold a candle to the exuberance of motherhood.

You can imagine the look on people's faces when I would respond: "Umm, it's not that much fun."

If you're reading this, chances are you've figured out that life with a baby is a total mind bender. Of course, it's this blessed journey you're wildly grateful for, but it also feels like you got blindsided by a freight train. Right?

Honestly, you kinda did. The mayhem of motherhood is an experience like none other.

When I became a mom in October 2014, as a thirty-two-year-old woman with a successful, decade-long career, it completely flipped my world upside down. Prior to my daughter's birth, I read all the standard-fare baby books recommended by friends and family; I wanted to be as ready as possible for her arrival, so I armed myself with any gadget or tidbit of knowledge that promised to make life with a newborn a bit easier.

Like most moms-to-be, I was peppered with warnings about how "exhausted" and "hormonal" I'd be while juggling the responsibilities and realities of this new role, but I wasn't overly concerned. Women have managed to get through childbirth and infancy since the beginning of humankind; I was certain I could handle it. I mean, teen moms were figuring it out, so, how hard could it be?

Apparently . . . really fucking hard.

Here's the thing: women today are more unprepared for motherhood than at any other point in history (save for, like, the Stone Age). That may seem like a bold statement, but I stand by it.

Sure, you've seen some of your friends and family become mothers, and they probably assured you that motherhood has awakened their soul. Maybe they even told you that motherhood has filled their heart beyond measure and that from the moment their child was born a supernatural maternal instinct began pulsating through their veins.

I'm sorry to tell you this, but people lie. Not all people, but enough people.

Look, I know you probably have that best friend from high school who always kept it real, who told you how pathetic it looked when you kept calling that guy (guilty!), but when she had a baby, she failed to mention just how hard it could be.

Lying by omission is still lying. To be fair, she was most likely trying to protect you or saying what she could to keep her own head above water, because, honestly, motherhood is gonna come at you like a thief in the night. You never had a chance, because you never saw it comin'.

As modern women, we are simply ill-equipped to transition from independent boss lady to mommy-mommy-mommy. It sounds counterintuitive because we are more educated, more successful, and more motivated than any generation past, but that's precisely the point.

Becoming a mother is a natural life event, but it doesn't always come *naturally*. Actually, it can feel really unnatural, especially in the beginning. For many new moms, it's an upheaval of the status quo. In becoming mothers, we're asked to give up a lot: our bodies, our identities, our priorities, our sanity, and, for some of us, our jobs. Motherhood isn't easy, but at some point we started treating it like it is, because we just stopped preparing ourselves for it.

Maybe that's the cost of being the "girl power" generation? Don't get me wrong, I believe wholeheartedly in raising strong girls to be whoever and whatever they want, because for most of history that wasn't the case. More and more, girls today are taught to aspire beyond motherhood to create meaningful, fulfilling, and powerful existences not predetermined by our gender.

Take me, for example. As a little girl, I wanted to pursue an oh-so-sexy career as a paleontologist. I carried around a Strawberry Shortcake suitcase filled with dinosaur books. I never really played "house" with my friends or pushed baby dolls around in a stroller. I don't even think I had many baby dolls, but that was mostly because I had an older brother who found joy in destroying my toys. He once melted the face off my Ken doll with a lighter; it was a real low point.

Even in school, young people are no longer taught "the domestic arts," which I think could serve *all* kids well, boys and girls. Think about it: When's the last time you heard of anyone taking a home ec class? I sure as hell never took one. While writing this, I googled how to bake chicken (seriously, though, multitasking is my life).

Outside of school, my own mother (a stay-at-home mom for eighteen years) encouraged my studies, my sports, and even my eccentric dreams of paleontology. She wanted more for me than she felt she had as a young woman, and I don't think that's uncommon. For many twenty- and thirtysomethings today, our mothers were a generation stuck somewhere between June Cleaver and Katy Perry, so they wanted to arm us with what they believed we needed most: fierce ambition and unwavering confidence.

My mom never schooled me on what to do in case of severe diaper rash or the art of removing breast milk stains. (She wouldn't have been able to help in this department anyway, because she never breastfed. To hear her tell it, "it seemed sort of barbaric." You'll learn more about her later. She's actually the best—and the worst.) The bottom line is that she didn't want to *assume* I'd be a mother or didn't want me to believe that it was my life's sole purpose, and I'm grateful to her for that. But in her attempt to raise a "hear me roar" kind of girl, I missed out on some of those important lessons that could have served me well when my daughter was born.

Many of us grew up believing that motherhood wasn't the *only* thing we'd do with our lives. That's not to say we didn't have an aunt, a mother-in-law, or a grandmother who routinely asked passive-aggressive questions about our childbearing decisions or who made off-color comments about our age, but, for the most part, it was generally accepted that we could be multifaceted. Motherhood was just one of many life buckets to fill, not the only one.

The bummer is that in creating this "new normal" for women—which is important—we've forfeited much of that generational passing down of knowledge. And that's a real loss, because no matter how evolved we become in society, we're still the only sex with the ability to push human life out of our lower torso.

All this raises the question: How the hell are women today supposed to know what to do when a baby does come along? We expect ourselves to tackle motherhood with the same self-sufficient gusto we exhibit in our pre-baby lives and, therefore, when shit hits the fan (or, in my case, the bookshelf, rug, rocker . . . basically anywhere in a three-foot radius of the changing table), we don't think to ask for help. We have long embraced the "I can do it all" mentality and anticipate motherhood being just another trophy in our armoire of impressive, fought-for accomplishments. Those are some pretty ambitious expectations for any woman to have of herself, let alone a new mom.

For many women with strong personal and professional identities, becoming a mother causes a complete restructuring of their life. Those early days are a total whirlwind cloaked in sleep deprivation, tear stains, and constant second-guessing. Minutes somehow feel like hours, but days often come and go so quickly we have no idea whether it's Tuesday or Friday. Time itself becomes entirely subjective, and defined edges cease to exist.

Having a child is an incredibly fulfilling life experience, but that's not a conclusion many come to overnight. Truth? Caring for a baby can be a struggle, especially in the beginning. I've always loved my daughter, certainly, but I didn't actually *enjoy* her until she got a bit older. It's hard to enjoy something you feel like you're failing at. Saying that may make me sound like an asshole to some people, but it also is honest . . . and when it comes to motherhood, I don't think my putting on a pretense helps anyone.

Every moment of my new existence was about Tallulah: she demanded all of my attention, all of my energy, and even my body was a vehicle for her well-being. It's not just that my needs took a backseat to my daughter's; they weren't even allowed in the car. No longer was I an individual; I was a mother. And somewhere in the dark recesses of my brain, I became resentful. I was someone before I became a mom, but as days became weeks, and weeks became months, I couldn't always remember who that was.

I found myself reminiscing about life before baby: impromptu movie nights, weekend hikes with my husband, reading a book that wasn't about sleep schedules, having a second glass of wine without having to strip to test the blood-alcohol level in my breast milk. I even fantasized about work! What I would have given to spend a few hours away from the mind-numbing routine of feed, clean, change, rock, repeat. And in the dark fog of the long nights, I found myself wishing for something a new mom could never possibly admit out loud: my old life back.

To make matters worse, from where I stood, it truly seemed like I was the only new mama struggling. Every time I scrolled through social media, I stumbled upon countless photos of moms who seemed to be relishing new motherhood. Each image was a version of the same: a beautiful mama, her hair pulled into a chunky boho braid that revealed flawless skin, resting in a fluffy bed of pillows and gazing down at her sleeping newborn.

Platforms like Facebook and Instagram yielded to this new parenting superbreed: the unicorn mom, the picture-perfect women who appear to be thriving in their new roles and whose photos always seem to say: "Don't mind me, folks. I'm just over here *owning* motherhood. What? Like it's supposed to be hard?" And for whatever reason, these women have unjustly become the measure by which all new mamas grade themselves—and one another. It's propagated a social media culture hell-bent on holding women to unrealistic standards. This is where shit can go from difficult to dangerous.

I spent my days covered in spit-up and sweat stains, not hazy, dreamy, blush-toned filters. My child went through a super adorable baby acne phase, and my unwashed topknot didn't nail that "messy glamour" look. Bearing witness to the seemingly authentic experiences of other new mothers left me feeling devalued, anxious, and unsuccessful.

Only one thing was certain: when it came to mom life, I was totally blowing it. I was failing my daughter; she deserved better. The moment she arrived I fell madly in love with her (which isn't actually very common; I attribute my experience to the morphine), which made my feelings of inadequacy and self-doubt that much worse. I wanted the best for my baby. The more difficult my struggle became, the more defeated I felt.

I mean . . . how *did* those "teen moms" do it? Even though these girls shouldn't necessarily be the barometer of sound parenting, I'd venture to guess that their lack of worldly experience actually works to their benefit in this particular arena. Of her own experience as a young mother my mom said, "Having a baby isn't all that life-changing when you don't have much of a life to give up."

It appeared that my success was my downfall. I was so established and rooted in who I was as a human that motherhood upended everything I had ever known about myself. This new world was nothing like the one I spent all that time building for myself, and it appeared to be a very lonely, unfamiliar place. I was like a castaway trying to survive—without the emotional shoulder of a Wilson volleyball.

It's clear to me now—with the benefit of hindsight and a full night's sleep—that what I desperately needed was support. I needed to feel the compassion and honesty of other women, not the judgment or burden of impossible expectations. I needed to know that my struggle was not singular. I needed the safety of a community there to guide me through this time. And, mostly, I needed my own mom. But like many of my generational peers, I had moved away from home when I set off to pursue my career. Even though I was just ninety minutes north of my parents' house, I didn't have that "she's just around the corner" comfort many new moms crave.

Think about it: members of today's nuclear family are more likely to be farther geographical distances from their kin—or comparable community—than at any other point in history, which in turn leaves many first-time mothers without the inherent support we need during our transition.

In many ancient cultures, people would band together to help new mothers recover from pregnancy and delivery and to comfort women as they adjusted to their new life. It's why people say, "It takes a village." It's a cliché, but clichés exist for a reason. Even through the mid-twentieth century, extended families remained neighbors, sometimes living within blocks of one another, like my mother's family on the South Side of Chicago, where four sisters lived on the same street, along with their own mom.

Traditionally, new mothers relied on the other women in their tribe to encourage them, comfort them, and help them. The absence of such communities has, in part, contributed to the rise in popularity of antepartum and postpartum service providers—like doulas, pregnancy coaches, and night nurses—particularly in urban areas, where more women tend to be farther removed from their families.

Sufficiently terrified? I swear there's a payout, but before going further, let me say this again: I love my daughter to the ends of the earth. My baby girl is the best thing I've ever done. When she was small, I'd often cry to my husband (after a glass or three of wine) about how I've never done anything that has made me worthy enough to deserve her, and I truly believe it. The next morning, she'd shit in my hand and our cosmic balance was restored. (For the record, yes, this actually happened. Every single anecdote in this book is 100 percent real, no matter how far-fetched.)

At the end of the day, my apparent mental collapse wasn't really because of my sweet baby. She was an innocent little human going through some major adjustments of her own as she got familiar with the world around her and her own small body. This craziness was about me and my struggle becoming a mom.

Recognizing that was the first step in managing it all.

As I write, my daughter is four years old and has grown into this amazing little girl I absolutely adore (save for the occasional toddler meltdowns that most recently included a pair of salad tongs thrown at my head and a roar to "get out" of my own home). Since coming through my daughter's infancy, I've spent countless hours with friends, family, and even the sister of my favorite Starbucks barista, talking to them about this transition. I can actually see the relief in their eyes when I say something they never hear: "It sucks sometimes, right?"

We're made to believe that feeling overwhelmed or ill-prepared isn't allowed. As if it would somehow reflect poorly on us if we were to admit that having a child is more demanding than we ever thought possible; therefore, no one talks about it. We bottle it up—our anxieties, our fears, and our feelings of self-doubt—and hide behind a forced smile. We save our breakdowns for the moments when we're alone. We're convinced that other new moms aren't struggling as much as we are, and that must mean we are terrible mothers.

Mamas, rest assured that no matter the day you had, someone has walked that path before and someone will soon follow. I can say with certainty that some other mom has forgotten to buckle her newborn into the car seat before jumping on the freeway and that some other mom has had to call the pediatrician because she threw up in her baby's mouth. I know for a fact that some other mom has gone to pick up Chinese food, only to return to a screaming infant that she accidentally left alone, and that some other mom inadvertently used breast milk to make her husband's smoothie (my husband questions just how "inadvertent" this mistake really was). I know that some other mom has piled up newborn diapers on the driver's seat of her car in order to relieve herself, just to avoid having to go back into the mall with a fussy infant.

And I know without a doubt that some other mom has poured herself a glass of wine, well before noon, and retreated to the garage to weep loudly while listening to Taylor Swift (only to be interrupted by a neighbor who decided to investigate the source of "those alarming sobs"), and once you find a way to manage this incredible transition, you'll discover that being a mom is, yes, the hardest, most rewarding thing you'll ever do.

Having a baby is a soul-defining experience that will forever change a woman's life. So, I have to wonder, when did we ever start believing that something so monumental could ever be so easily managed?

While walking the crazy motherhood tightrope, I believe it is fundamental that we, as women, understand what a shit show new motherhood can be. But I am here to assure you that things will get easier, that you will absolutely get through it, and that you are not alone. There is great comfort in knowing that you can have a hard time—a really hard time—and still be a fucking awesome mom.

And . . . you are.

THE BIRTH OF A MOTHER

2

"Loofah your nipples."

Certain I misheard, I chalked it up to pregnancy brain and asked my friend to repeat herself.

"Start loofah-ing your nipples," she explained, with alarming nonchalance. "You need to rough them up so they start to callus."

Reading what had to be a look of total confusion smeared across my face, she clarified: "When you're in the shower, just . . . scrub them." She raised an arm over her head, salad fork still in hand, and began miming the motion. My eyes darted around the patio of the Beverly Hills café, making sure no one I knew was here to witness my friend faux groom herself. I was desperately hoping to salvage our glamorous "ladies who lunch" moment, but she clearly didn't get the memo. She put her arm down and concluded, "You know . . . for breastfeeding."

She hadn't bothered to ask whether I was planning to breastfeed; she just assumed that I would be. After all, what kind of monster chooses to formula feed her baby? In Los

Angeles, it felt like there were few greater sins than not exclusively breastfeeding your child, which made me an outsider because I wasn't entirely sold on the concept and my friend's suggestion to use a coarse sponge to toughen up the skin tissue on my breasts wasn't exactly helping. Breastfeeding is not for the weak of heart. I'll dive more into this later, but it can be a challenging road, and I had witnessed friends struggle with the pain, the pressure, and the all-encompassing nature of it. Your body isn't your own, and I just kept thinking about how anxious I was to get back to *me* as soon as possible.

Throughout my pregnancy, I felt like a visitor in my own skin. Despite the extra thirty-five pounds hanging around my midsection, I felt totally disconnected. And feeling like a different person physically and emotionally became really confusing for me mentally. I spent three decades being one person, and pregnancy was forcing me to become someone else. Does that even make sense? I just kept telling myself that it was all temporary. I foolishly assumed that after pregnancy, I would return to who I was before baby. Sure, life would be hectic for a while, but at least I would feel like myself again. Right?

So wrong.

Even though I was going through the motions of planning for a baby to join our family, I had no way of predicting my own personal metamorphosis and, therefore, had no reason to plan for the disaster I couldn't see coming. Sure, everyone told me my world was about to flip upside down, but it was usually an off-the-cuff remark said with a laugh. I didn't take it too seriously. So, I checked off nursery "must-have" lists and scoured sample registries to prepare for having a baby, but did absolutely nothing to prepare myself for motherhood.

Since announcing my pregnancy, like many expectant moms, I was on the receiving end of much advice, but no one talked to me about how challenging a woman's journey can be in becoming a mother—save for my sister, who appeared slightly concerned about this new venture and asked whether I was certain I wanted "to do this" (she's the mom of two boys, two years apart, and has been exhausted since 2006). The rest of the sweeping suggestions I learned to take with a grain of salt. There's nothing particularly helpful in being told to "sleep when the baby sleeps," "take care of yourself," or, the biggest offender, "enjoy every minute." And some of the more practical, grounded advice got lost in the postpartum fog of war. I was just trying to get through the days without my baby falling out (toward the end, I was convinced that I was one sneeze away from crowning, despite my doctor's assurances that it couldn't happen).

I also started to despise dismissive and passively condescending commentary like "just you wait" and "you'll see!" I felt like I had already paid forward some substantial motherhood dues and didn't appreciate being made to feel like an idiot because my baby was still inside my body instead of out. Maybe I hadn't yet experienced a sleepless night or the cutting of a tooth, but my body had already pushed itself to physical boundaries I was unaware existed. For that reason alone, I expected to get some sort of credit in the mama department. After all, my growing belly was responsible for splitting up Crosby, Stills and Nash (again), as each member pictured on my vintage rock T-shirt were pulled into different area codes across my ever-widening stomach.

I have to be honest—if it isn't already painfully clear—I had a very difficult time with pregnancy. It's a shit thing to have to say because I know my daughter might someday read this (I love YOU, Tallulah. I just didn't love feeling like my organs were going to expel out of my vagina and plummet to the earth). The physical and mental toll of growing a human was a lot. Pregnancy is hard. It's hard on our bodies, our hormones, as well as our emotional health. It can make getting through our daily routine feel like an Iron Man race, even during the easiest of pregnancies. It's no wonder I was so eager to get back to feeling like my pre-baby self.

THINGS THAT SUCK WHILE YOU'RE PREGNANT

» ***Weddings:*** I went to four while pregnant. At the first two, no one knew I was pregnant. I spent one evening drinking ginger ale out of a champagne glass, and the other avoiding a particularly sloppy groomsman who was for some reason determined to dance with me (and nearly knocked me to the ground a few times). One of my best friends got married a few weeks before my due date, and it was probably the nicest wedding I've ever been to. Feeling sorry for myself, I spent most of the reception sitting at my table eating an entire apple pie. With an open bar and trays of champagne, dirty martinis, and margaritas offered, my husband proceeded to get so drunk that I found him huffing on an American Spirit cigarette (he doesn't smoke) and attempting to start a mosh pit to the band's performance of Katy Perry's "Firework." (Despite his denials, I can attest that this report is 100 percent accurate.)

» ***Bikini waxes:*** You ever try getting a Brazilian in your third trimester? It's ungodly. Between the sheer force of gravity and the increased blood flow, that entire region is like a bundle of live wires. I hadn't seen my vagina in weeks, so why the hell did I put myself through that anyway? For the OB? I'm pretty sure if my husband and I were having sex, we were both shutting our eyes and praying for it to be over. I gave waxing a college try, but abandoned the effort and embraced my inner flower child for much of my third trimester.

» ***Nipples:*** Did you know that you can start producing and expelling milk before your child is born? It's a super fun party trick, especially when you're halfway through a dim sum brunch and mowing down a truffle pork dumpling. It's not just a drop, either. By this point, your nipples are likely the size of slices of salami, with coloring to match (nurses insist that this is so the baby can find the nipple, but I don't know how the hell they could miss it), so those suckers are capable of producing some pretty decent fluid pressure.

- *Pumping gas:* At eight months pregnant, I struggled to understand my physical dimensions. So much so that while fueling my car, my belly knocked the gas hose out of the tank. About a gallon of gas shot up in the air and came raining down on me. I spent the next five hours down an internet rabbit hole and was surprised to learn that many women before me had wondered about the "harms of gasoline exposure to an unborn child."
- *Pre-baby piercings:* I never thought I would live to see the day I would admit my mother might have been right about something, but by my third trimester, I was definitely rethinking that circa 1999 belly button piercing. I mean, wow . . . that was a really awesome decision. The tiny little hole where the barbell once lived was now the size of a large oval. I was convinced that with enough force I could squeeze a grape through it.
- *Physical movement:* During the final weeks of pregnancy, it was difficult to walk more than twenty uninterrupted feet—except when an ice cream truck broke down at the end of the street, in which case, you've never seen a pregnant bitch move so fast. Otherwise, walking upstairs became an Olympic sport reserved solely for bedtime, with the support of my husband, who anchored himself behind me and pushed; I was both grateful and wildly resentful of this. I peed approximately every ninety minutes and therefore spent most nights watching infomercials that promised to work magic on my soon-to-be-destroyed postpartum hair. Later in this book, I talk a lot about postpartum hormones, but let us not forget how INSANE prenatal ones can be. My pregnancy hormones had completely taken over the part of my brain that housed common sense and reason. Without warning, I would routinely erupt into hysterics over things like the mistreatment of Caesar in *Planet of the Apes* or the fact that we had yet to buy a deep freezer for our garage. I sobbed uncontrollably in the passenger seat of my husband's car until he agreed to abandon his Sunday football plans to drive me to a Sears in the San

Fernando Valley. (Looking back, my tears had more to do with the fact that we had just bumped into Jennifer Lopez at a pumpkin patch in West Hollywood. She looked like a radiant, glowing angel in perfectly fitted white jeans. She tossed a few pumpkins into the back of her Bentley drop-top, and I couldn't help but feel sorry for myself.)

To be fair, one of my favorite people in the world, my friend Aili, is obsessed with pregnancy. She has three kids and enjoyed each of her experiences. That's a lie: she didn't enjoy them, she *loved* them. I remember sitting at her house the day before she went in to deliver her first child and she was legit mourning the fact that she wouldn't be pregnant anymore. While pregnant with her second child, she decided, on a whim, to fly to Israel to float in the Dead Sea. She embraces pregnancy and relishes it. She's a unicorn human.

IN DEFENSE OF PREGNANCY

Yes, despite the weight gain, fatigue, that insane pressure when your belly hangs lower than you thought possible, and two very painful bouts of sciatica, I loved being pregnant. I loved watching my babies grow inside me, sensing them flip and dip and kick. I loved feeling more feminine and more powerful than ever before. My body was creating a living, breathing human being, one that would be connected to me for the rest of my life!

Plus, it was pretty fantastic to be able to eat Trader Joe's Chocolate Covered Cherries by the carton without feeling any guilt.

Also, a pregnant woman gets so much kind attention: compliments, offers to help, a seat when it's crowded, and so on. At eight months pregnant with my third child, a very nice man not only helped me out of the grocery and loaded my car but also went back into the store to buy me a case of water when I realized I had forgotten to get one.

For me, pregnancy was the easy part; it's the aftermath that was the wake-up call!

—Aili Nahas, journalist and mom of three

I'm sure lots of moms feel like Aili—just not *all* moms. As mothers-to-be, we are constantly bombarded with the reminder that creating life is a woman's sacred rite. Because of that, some people feel that we should just shut up and appreciate this blessing, that we should just quit bemoaning our aches and pains because, for many women, conceiving a child is a painful struggle and our flippant attitudes can be seen as disrespectful or lacking compassion. The women who have trouble conceiving would give anything to experience the struggle of pregnancy, and, therefore, we shouldn't complain about our cankles. I understand that argument intimately because I struggled to get pregnant with my son (and spent much of my pregnancy on bed rest for fear of losing him).

That being said, I don't understand how my not enjoying all the crazy shit that happens to our bodies in any way means that I'm not incredibly grateful for the little human being growing inside me. Even before struggling with my second pregnancy, I still had sincere respect for what my body was capable of. When I was expecting my daughter, I vividly remember the incredible anxiety I felt at each doctor's appointment. I would shut my eyes and hold my breath during every ultrasound, waiting to hear that little heartbeat, and would feel my stomach churning as we awaited test results. And I knew what a blessing it was to find out that she was perfect; she has fingers, eyeballs, and a central nervous system, all of which she developed while living inside me. I appreciated *her*; I just didn't happen to love the sudden appearance of jawline acne or the erratic bursts of emotion for no actual reason or the fact that tying my shoelaces required cutting off blood flow to the bottom half of my body. I don't believe one begets the other.

Pregnancy can feel super weird, especially for a first-time mom, and, if I'm being honest, I think my general displeasure with it was bigger than just the physical challenges and the daily dance with hormones. I was growing someone new, and somewhere in my subconscious I must have known I was becoming someone new, which meant I needed to say goodbye to the woman I spent thirty-two years being. I just didn't realize all of this at the time, so, instead of preparing for my own transformation on top of stockpiling diapers and burp cloths, I kept telling myself that I'd get back to "being myself" soon.

I knew friends who had been through the transition into their mom roles and had seen enough movies to understand that life was about to get messy, but I couldn't *feel* it . . . not enough to really wrap my head around what was happening. What would it be like to see her for the first time? Would I fall in love with her? How would it feel to bring her home? What kind of mom would I be? Would I know when my maternal instincts kicked in?

I didn't know the answer, so I did what I always do when I'm petrified: over-research, overanalyze, and overthink. I studied and read everything I could find on infant care to the point of total neurosis. I cross-referenced at least a dozen nursery checklists to make sure I wasn't missing a single item. It didn't take a therapist to figure out that I was compensating for my deep insecurity. I planned for the business of becoming a mom, because I was so nervous about actually becoming someone's mother.

Where was the pre-baby checklist for navigating this shit, huh?!

Why didn't I know that pregnancy wasn't just about me growing and developing a baby but also about growing and preparing myself to become a mom? Why wasn't this covered in all those baby books or the baby prep classes at the hospital?

The postpartum identity struggle that many women experience in the early weeks and months is born during pregnancy, which is why it often feels so severe when we actually realize what's going on. By the time our children are eight months old, we may have been disconnected with our sense of self for a year and a half already. Kardashian Kulture teaches us that pregnancy is temporary, but, really, it's the start of a forever change.

Developing my new identity as "mama" didn't start when I had my daughter, as I imagined it would; it began when I got pregnant. Those forty weeks weren't just a sacred time for my child to develop and grow inside my body as she readied herself for the outside world; they were also a period of time when I should have been getting ready for my own transition into new motherhood. While my body was preparing itself for my new role, I should have spent more time readying my mind. I was embarking on this sacred journey, where I would willingly surrender much of myself for this child, and pregnancy was nature's way of letting me know that the train had left the station. Instead of asking other moms which diaper pail they used or whether or not they would recommend getting a wipes warmer, I wish I would have asked them about what they felt they could have benefited from in those early days.

I was prepared for the expected, but that's not where motherhood is actually born. Real motherhood happens in the tear-filled, sleepless nights when you're left alone to wonder where the hell it all went wrong. I was so terrified that I would be a shitty mom to this child I already loved so much that I figured I could make up for my lack of maternal instincts by being over-studied. If I knew the answers, I was convinced that the test itself wouldn't be that hard. I was hoping that my being overprepared would translate into being a good enough mom for my baby.

Wow, did I miss the entire fucking point or what? I failed to plan for what *my* needs were going to be in the days, weeks, and months ahead of this huge transition (which I discuss in more depth in Chapter 3). Mother Nature gets us halfway there, but it's up to us to do the rest of the work. It's like gymnastics: your approach usually dictates whether you'll stick the landing. Most of us are so off course by the time baby arrives that we never really had a fighting chance, which is why I believe I struggled so much with my own issues of identity those first few months. We're already at such a deficit that it's impossible to catch up.

Of course, the books and checklists would help keep my sanity, but being a great mother had nothing to do with the number of swaddle options I had and more to do with being in the best mind-set, ready for this new person to join our family.

All the advice thrust upon me during my pregnancy reminded me how hard babies could be, but I didn't understand how much more difficult new motherhood would become when I was simultaneously experiencing sleep deprivation and a hormone imbalance, while also recovering from childbirth. As the mama, I'm the one in charge of holding it all together, but how could I possibly do that when I wasn't able to hold myself together?

Although I can't go back in time and make up for all those things now, recognizing just how blindly I wandered into this new chapter can better help me understand why I struggled as much as I did. It allows me the opportunity to forgive myself for my less-than-stellar moments, of which there were quite a few, and to remind myself that my experience is in no way a reflection of just how much I love the amazing little girl who now rules my world. We're so hard on ourselves because becoming a mother is serious business with critical consequences, and, hopefully, recognizing that we weren't really prepared for it can afford us a bit of grace.

Looking back, my friend's insane suggestion was probably the best advice I received during my pregnancy. Yes, it was crazy, but that's the thing: new motherhood is fucking crazy.

If I would have listened to her, I probably wouldn't have had such a horrendous time breastfeeding those first few weeks, which meant

I wouldn't have felt like such a disappointment when it all fell to pieces. If callusing my boobs with a loofah would have helped me avoid feeling paralyzing anxiety whenever it was time to feed, I would have happily managed any temporary discomfort.

Thinking about our lunch and how out of place and oblivious I thought my friend was, I get now that I was actually the one who was totally clueless. It wasn't that she was unaware of social graces—she just didn't give a fuck. Her priorities were different; the shit she cared about was different. She was *already* a mom. She was born into motherhood and she had the experience that I wasn't yet privy to.

Maybe we can't properly explain this transition to women who are expecting. I mean, who wants to be Debbie Downer at the baby shower, shoving macaroons in her face and telling the mama-to-be that a perineal tear is nothing compared to the tearing apart of your soul when you've been forced to listen to Baby Shark for the ten-thousandth time? I can't imagine that news going over well. Instead, we offer a "just you wait," and keep alive the vicious cycle.

But maybe it's up to us, the mamas who have been there, to rally around new mothers. Maybe it's our duty to welcome them into this beautiful, messy new chapter of life and to let them know that they have gone through their own rebirth. Perhaps we can give them the comfort of knowing that a community of moms who have been down this road before will support them and empathize with them as they struggle with the new duality of their existence.

Maybe that's what my friend was trying to do, but I was too worried about her salad fork waving to recognize it.

PREPARING FOR THE POSTPARTUM MIND FUCK

Prep for In-Home Self-Care

No matter how many times someone warns you about how drastically your life will change, it doesn't really hit home until the baby arrives. Carving out any time for self-care is damn near impossible with a newborn, so prepare ahead of time to give yourself a fighting chance. Hit up Target and pick up a bunch of sheet masks for in-home facials or treat yourself to a few new nail polish colors. Download some podcasts to have on tap in case you can sneak out for a walk, and invest in comfy postpartum clothes that you feel good in.

Journal

As a writer, I'm a big advocate of keeping a journal. It gives me an opportunity to check in with myself and to be honest about how I'm feeling. Not to mention, writing feels pretty cathartic. Plus, if it becomes a habit during pregnancy, you can keep journaling through the early postpartum period, when checking in with yourself is even more critical (but that might just be wishful thinking).

Make a Pre-Baby Bucket List

Recognizing that having a baby is an incredible—and relatively permanent—lifestyle change is important to readying yourself for this transition. It also means saying goodbye to much of your pre-baby life. That being said, don't be afraid to take a victory lap! Sit down with your partner and make a list of a few things you really want to do before baby is here. Check out a new art exhibit; watch *Gone with the Wind;* try the new hipster Korean BBQ spot . . . you get the idea. For me, I wanted to organize the garage and get my house in order. It was not that glamorous, but it definitely helped me manage the chaos.

Talk to Other Moms

A large reason why many of us feel so blindsided by new motherhood is because we spend much of our pregnancy planning for the baby, not planning for ourselves. We ask for recommendations on strollers and swings and swaddles, but don't ask for insight into what we will go through and feel like in those early days. Ask other mothers about their experience, and be open to hearing about their journeys.

Assemble Your Mom Army

I talk about this a lot, but plan to have support around you, and in your home, as much as possible in the days and weeks after baby is born. Part of the reason many of us go insane is because we are left on our own to navigate this new world. Your ego might balk at the idea of your mother-in-law coming to town for two weeks or asking your mother to sleep on the couch, but just trust me on this one. I never needed my mom more than when I became a mom.

3

YOU WERE NOT PREPARED FOR THIS: THE POSTPARTUM RITE OF PASSAGE

"How are you so calm?"

I looked over and saw a panic-stricken woman gaping at me from her wheelchair. My husband and I had just arrived at the Labor & Delivery registration desk at Cedars-Sinai Medical Center in Los Angeles. It was five fifteen in the morning, but we were wide awake and continued our conversation from the car ride over (debating fan theories on *The Walking Dead*, a television show about the zombie apocalypse).

To someone on the outside, I must imagine that I looked relatively civilized. I had the luxury of knowing our birth schedule, so I got my hair blown out the evening before and even indulged in a predelivery manicure (this is the sort of shit we do in LA). And unlike most mamas-to-be, I was able to walk into the hospital, not having spent the last few hours hunched over with crippling contractions. All in all, I'd successfully avoided the realities I was about to come face-to-face with.

"Don't worry," I said to her, with a laugh. "I'm actually in total denial right now."

It was meant to be a joke, but it couldn't have been more true. My birth plan was short and sweet: drugs by any means necessary. I had managed to evade learning much about what my delivery would be like (on purpose), because I wasn't entirely sure I could handle it.

SHIT YOU SHOULD KNOW: BIRTH PLANS

Unlike me, lots of moms-to-be take a fair amount of time to research and create their childbirth plan, as responsible, noncynical parents-to-be. In researching this book, I spent a good deal of time talking with gynecologists and obstetricians. The conservative consensus is this: about 80 percent of all deliveries do not go exactly to an expectant parent's birth plan. Eighty percent! That's not to say the entire birth plan will be obsolete but that certain aspects will have to be adjusted.

While it's still a good idea to have a birth plan in place, just keep in mind that babies have their own ideas about how they'd like to enter the world and, more importantly, recognize the possibility that you need to be flexible. It's a lot easier to prepare yourself for the idea now than it is when you're eight centimeters dilated and chewing on ice chips. Instead of developing a birth plan that you and your partner are married to, instead think of it as "birth preferences."

Things to include: your medical history; the names and contact info of family members; your preferences for drugs and pain management, episiotomies, birthing positions, placenta preservation, cord banking, and so forth; and your wishes for newborn care and your postpartum care (skin-to-skin, breastfeeding, first bath, and any state-mandated vaccines or medications for baby).

As my due date fast approached, I developed symptoms of preeclampsia. My doctor was monitoring the amount of protein in my urine, which meant that I had to drive around Los Angeles with an oversized jug of my own pee buckled into the passenger seat of my car. For twenty-four hours, I needed to collect all of my urine, so everywhere I went, my jug came with me. And do I need to remind you how much a thirty-nine-week-pregnant woman pees? I even tried to take the jug into a restaurant for one last pre-baby dinner with a friend, but my husband thought I'd be violating some pretty major health code laws.

A week before my due date, with the symptoms still present, my doctor advised that it was time to get the baby out, and we had a decision to make: induction or C-section. The doctor told me that my daughter was measuring on the larger side and that her head was not yet engaged in the birth canal (basically, she was a big, stubborn baby). This meant that inducing labor could prove challenging, which I took as "you might end up in surgery anyway." My husband and I (but mostly me) decided to opt for the caesarean.

I know it's not the choice everyone would make, but to hear my doctor tell it, it sounded less dramatic. I would get to the hospital at five a.m. and the baby would be out by seven that morning. It took longer to get my hair colored! Was I scared? Of course! The very idea of labor and delivery terrified me—regardless of which way this baby would come out. Not only was getting the baby out quickly a priority for my doctor, it also meant that I was guaranteed the good drugs. (For the record, I know people have very strong opinions on drugs during labor. It's a deeply personal choice, and I respect wholeheartedly the mama warriors who choose to go all natural. I wasn't one of them, but I'm sure those mamas will respect my decisions too.)

But like I said, my knowledge about what would actually occur was limited. I knew I'd be awake for the procedure and that a giant sheet would block me from seeing what was happening to all my organs as the baby was removed through an incision in my lower abdomen. The night before delivery, my husband and I watched an episode of a reality TV show in which the star delivered her child by C-section. That was the extent of our prep. Learning anything beyond what was suitable for a television audience was unnecessary. Because I wasn't having a vaginal birth, my doctor would do most of the heavy lifting. I figured I'd recover in the hospital for a few days, be sent home with some painkillers, and that was it. Pregnancy over. It seems insane, especially considering how diligent I was about researching things like organic mattress covers and cool-mist humidifiers, but I think it had a lot to do with self-preservation.

During pre-op, my husband and I continued doing what we do best—masking our anxiety with humor. We joked about how the surgical suit made him look like Walter White and how my newly diagnosed "rolling veins"—discovered after it took four different nurses to get an IV going—meant that I could never develop an intravenous drug habit.

"It's go time," my obstetrician announced gleefully at 7:35 a.m. Apparently, she had had to jockey for an operating room and we had a small window to get in there before it got snatched up. The nurse helped me out of my bed and escorted me, by the elbow, into the OR.

Walking into the cold, sterile space felt unnerving. In the movies, women are always rolled on beds into the delivery room, and that sort of entrance felt far more fitting (I also much preferred to be heavily sedated). The nurse directed me to take a seat on the end of the operating table, and I noticed my husband was no longer by my side. Reading my mind, the nurse pointed to the hall where he had been instructed to wait until beckoned for. A few more doctors and nurses appeared, and I became acutely aware of the commotion happening behind me but was advised to keep looking forward.

My pulse started to race, and a cool terror washed over my body as I realized what was about to happen. In just a few minutes, these people were going to open my stomach and remove a small child. I felt scared, I felt alone, and I felt foolishly clueless. I really had no idea what was going to happen next. Why didn't I know? They say ignorance is bliss, but at this moment, ignorance just felt ignorant.

"Uh, is someone gonna give me something?" To this day, I'm not sure whether those words actually came out of my mouth or I just thought them. Either way, I needed someone to nail me with a dart gun, like, ASAP.

"Where did you meet your husband, again?" the OB asked casually, tapping her foot to the soft hums of steel drum reggae swirling around the operating room. (Later, I asked her about her choice in surgical music, and she told me she usually opts for some sexy R&B, but that felt a little "too adult" for a morning procedure.)

"Huh?" I replied, more than slightly annoyed. Without my routine Botox injections, I was again capable of making facial expressions that had escaped me for years.

"I forget what you told me," she said, a calm smile fixed on her thin, tanned face, framed by wispy brown hair. "Where did you meet?"

"College," I snapped, determined not to be distracted. The room was surprisingly frigid, and the scratchy hospital gown did little in the way of comfort. As I sat on the edge of the table, I could feel the anesthesiologist swab antibacterial gel across my lower spine.

I took a few deep breaths and reminded myself that most women barely felt the epidural, pushing from my mind that those women were also experiencing frequent, mind-bending contractions.

"I'm gonna count to three," the man behind me said. "One . . . two . . . thr—"

"OH, FUUUUCKKKK!" I bellowed, so loudly that I was certain I shook the walls.

I felt it. I really fucking felt it. And that was just the numbing shot. The epidural itself wasn't a piercing pain but rather a dull, sturdy pressure that pushed forcefully into my lower spine. This, I decided, was not a good idea.

"Deep breaths," a nurse said, as the forceful pressure continued.

And that was it. I was lowered to my back, and a blue fabric partition was drawn between my upper and lower halves. Immediately, I saw my husband's face, white as a ghost but smiling. (He later told me that he was so startled by my scream as he waited in the hallway that he nearly dropped his phone—while reading ESPN, naturally.)

Suddenly a bit drunk, I asked the anesthesiologist, "Am I gonna get something to keep me calm?"

"There's already a little morphine coming through," he whispered.

I nodded, happy with his response, and turned my eyes toward the ceiling. Instantly, a wave of nausea washed over me and I quickly sealed my lips together to avoid puking into my own mouth. He must have read my face.

"Nauseous?" he asked.

I nodded again, wide-eyed. I never considered that I might get sick from the anesthesia, but it's quite common. And when you're about to have your abdomen opened, the doctor doesn't want a patient dry heaving. It's bad for business to have your stomach lurching up and down during surgery.

Blurry-eyed, I watched as he quickly juggled tubes and bags of liquid; within seconds I felt the sensation pass. He tilted the bed a few degrees to the left so that if I did happen to vomit, it would be to the left and not down my own throat. It was the obstetric equivalent of positioning your drunk, passed-out friend on her side before returning to the party.

As instructed, my husband was ready with videos of our dog running in slow motion around a grass field and attempting, in vain, to catch a Frisbee. (Prior to having a child, my dog was the light and life of my world. He now lives underneath my bed to avoid being terrorized, and I have to remind myself to check on him every few days to make sure he's still breathing.)

HOW TO HANDLE THE PETS YOU THOUGHT YOU LOVED AS MUCH AS YOUR BABY

You love your dog or cat, right? You never imagined you could ever love anyone as much as you love the sweet, loyal animal that kisses your nose or curls up next to you on the couch. In many ways, your pet was your firstborn and probably the center of all your holiday cards before baby. (I used to take my dog to see Santa.) Well, I hate to break it to you, but there will be days you will forget your pet even exists. My dog, Archie, was my *child* . . . until I had an actual child. Nowadays I only catch glimpses of him as he scurries from room to room trying to avoid my four-year-old. Here are a few tips for managing your fur baby after having a *real* baby.

- When first introducing your pet to your baby, try to do it *outside* of the home. I'm not entirely sure why experts suggest this, but I think it has something to do with meeting on neutral turf.
- Whoever the pet is more attached to, make sure that person (whether it's you or your partner) takes time to properly greet him or her when arriving home from the hospital. Animals get jealous, too.
- People say to introduce the baby's smell to your pet before bringing your little one home; I had my husband do that and he said the dog just looked at him like, "What the hell am I supposed to do with this hat?" But it gave me a little peace of mind.
- Expect a bit of hesitation and some acting out. Animals recognize that the family dynamic has shifted and that they're no longer king or queen of the castle, so who can really blame them?

» Once you're comfortable moving again, think about wearing your baby and taking your dog out for a walk. It's great physical and mental exercise for you both! If you have a cat, don't walk him or her. That's just crazy. Cats on leashes. I don't get it.

» Invest in extra toys, treats, and, if possible, a local dog walker (or even the kid down the block looking to earn a few dollars). Tired pets are good pets. Bored pets chew all the baby teethers and pee in the nursery.

✣ ✣ ✣

My doctor, along with two nurses, began speaking in hushed, serious voices.

"It'll just be a few minutes," the anesthesiologist told us, a big grin on his face. (When I received my bill a few days later and saw how much he got paid for sticking a giant fucking needle in my back, I realized that he had every reason to smile.) I could feel the doctor pushing on the outside of my stomach in what I thought was an attempt to position the baby before making the incision. I figured I still had a few minutes before the procedure began.

Along with my husband, I giggled as my dog once again took a flying leap toward the white plastic disc, his mouth open, determined to receive it, only to miss by a good two feet and land with a thud.

"Okay, get your phone ready, Dad," the anesthesiologist encouraged. Was he really suggesting my husband tape the whole thing? I appreciated his enthusiasm, but I didn't need the entire procedure captured; I was more interested in the end result.

But before I could say a word, I heard her: a sweet, high-pitched, catastrophic, gorgeous, life-altering cry. Ladies and gentlemen, she had arrived.

My eyes darted from the phone to the top of the draped curtain, where I saw her: ruby red and puff-faced, with a full tuft of dark hair matted to a perfectly shaped head.

"I'd like you to meet your daughter," the doctor announced.

I sobbed. There she was: my heart outside my body. In a single moment, I loved this little girl more than anything on this planet. I would have jumped, headfirst, into a pit of snakes for this child . . . even though I'm pretty sure my small intestines were still outside my body. It didn't matter. She was everything to me now.

And just like that, I was a mom.

It wasn't until later that I realized the pressure I felt wasn't coming from outside; they were already well within my body. Less than four minutes after I was placed on my back, my daughter arrived.

Almost immediately she was handed off to an older, quite striking-looking raven-haired nurse—Angelica Huston–like. She carried the baby over to an examining table, and my husband darted between the plastic bassinet and me.

"Go," I encouraged, as the nurse beckoned for him to cut the cord. The nurse wrapped our daughter in a cozy flannel blanket covered with footprints and beamed as she handed this perfect little bundle to my husband.

For a moment, I stared at the reflection in the plastic bassinet, before diverting my gaze.

I love the movie Witches, I thought. *I wonder if it's on Netflix?* (The morphine was really kicking in now that the baby was out.)

"Is everything okay?" the anesthesiologist asked, as I lay looking up at the ceiling.

"Oh yes," I said.

"Are you still nauseous?"

"Nope," I said. Then I realized he was probably wondering why I was looking at the ceiling instead of at my newborn daughter. "Oh!" I said. "I can see the reflection of my stomach being sewn back together in the side of her bassinet."

He looked at me wide-eyed but didn't say a word. I turned my gaze back to the ceiling to avoid seeing the real-time crime scene happening just twelve inches to the south. Within moments, the bassinet was moved.

When my husband brought her over, under the gentle guidance of the nurse, I got a good look at the person who had been growing inside of me all this time. It was a miracle. This small little girl—who came in just over eight pounds—had already flipped our world upside down. She was the one responsible for all my craziness the past forty weeks. She was the reason for all the aches and pains, the sleepless nights, the truly abnormal swelling, and the fact that my ass was twice its size.

And I couldn't have cared less. I had her now. That's all I needed.

The first few hours were, perhaps, the most blissful experience of my life. We sat together in recovery, my little family and me, as Tallulah nursed for the first time (I'll talk more about my decision to breastfeed in Chapter 9). We debated each detail of her face and argued over who she looked like more—we agreed that she, thankfully, got my nose. For the better part of that first morning together, we oohed and ahhed over her every perfection.

Then, the morphine wore off. The nausea returned. And the reality of what my body had just endured, and the repercussions of that event, began taking shape.

Looking back, I didn't realize how lucky we were to have those two peaceful hours, because once the drugs began to subside I felt like I got hit by a bus. My reaction to the anesthesia was so severe that I couldn't sit upright until about ten hours after surgery, which made it challenging to hold my new baby. Fortunately, my husband and my best friend Krystal (who was thirty-seven weeks pregnant herself) took turns cuddling with Tallulah, while my own mother held back my hair as I vomited into a beige-y pink plastic tray. The only interaction Tallulah and I really had outside of recovery occurred when the lactation consultant emerged to attach her onto one of my smooth, very uncallused nipples.

I knew how important that early bonding was for both me and her, but I was just so sick. Thinking back, I get a little pissed that my doctor didn't warn me about the possible side effects. Would I have still chosen the same path? Probably. But if she would have said that localized anesthesia (which is offered during a vaginal birth as well) can routinely cause nausea, I would have told her that I get easily sick and we could have discussed ways to combat it. When I gave birth to my son, I told my doctor and she prescribed me an anti-nausea patch for behind my ear. It changed my entire experience (and, I believe, put me on a healthier postpartum path).

Back to Tallulah. After our third attempt at getting a proper latch, the nurse offered me a pair of breast shells to help keep my now raw nipples comfortable between feedings.

In the hours after surgery, I retained so much water that my nose temporarily tripled in size and my fingers looked like breakfast sausages, and my legs were wrapped in automatic compression socks that tightened and relaxed in intervals. At one point, a nurse straight up told me not to look in the mirror.

"It's only going to make you feel worse," she said. "It's not worth it."

Every time I coughed, sneezed, threw up, or laughed, hot pain pierced my abdomen.

Twelve hours after surgery, it was required that I get up and walk around. My mom held Tallulah as I used the empty bassinet as a walker. My husband followed slowly behind, dodging the random bags of fluids dangling off the silver IV trolley.

And that was just the first day.

I knew that having a baby was a major medical event, but I had no idea *how* serious. The first few days postpartum are incredibly intense and can really set the tone for your entire recovery, but there isn't much information out there. I only knew what I had seen in movies, and I never remember hearing a new mother tell her friend, "I feel like I had a bomb go off between my legs." Personally, I think it's because by the time the new mom is home or receiving visitors, she already has an entirely new list of shit to worry about. Because I didn't realize the toll it would take on my body, I didn't understand how to properly honor it as a major trauma.

However, I did quickly realize that there would be no "snapping back" to my old self anytime soon.

While still in the hospital, I wasn't actually capable of taking care of myself at all, which was foreign to me. As a woman, I prided myself on my autonomy, but I had suddenly become entirely dependent on the people around me. I hated feeling like that. My body and mind seemed to be working at about 50 percent capacity; I required the assistance of a nurse every time I had to use the bathroom, which felt demeaning and embarrassing. I'd shuffle to the bathroom in Pilates grip socks while pressing a pillow to my abdominal incision, only to have this complete stranger squirt me with water, pat me down, and hold a plastic tray beneath me to collect and measure my urine.

On the third night, tired of having a stranger up in my lady parts, I asked my husband if he wouldn't mind helping me. Never before had I felt so vulnerable in front of another person. I remember standing in the horrible fluorescent light, lifting my hospital gown, so he could kneel down to clean me, put on fresh hospital-grade mesh underwear, and tend to the incision that spanned the width of my body. I started to cry.

Purely for my benefit, he brushed off the experience as if this was our typical Friday night routine. I was fragile, but he pretended not to notice, and never was I more grateful for or more in love with this man.

Foolishly, I viewed my vulnerability as a sign of weakness and my fragility as feeble, when in reality I was a warrior recovering from an epic battle. When wounded soldiers return from the battlefield, do we cloak them in failure? No, we crown them as heroes for their valiant sacrifice! Why the hell aren't we doing the same for new mothers!? Either you just had a grenade go off in your vagina or you just had your stomach sliced open. If you ask me, that sounds a hell of a lot like going to war.

Unfortunately, we live in a culture that expects us to take it on the chin.

I've recently adopted the idea of no longer freely interchanging the terms *normal* and *common*. Women so often struggle with postpartum recovery that we've begun to accept the pain and discomfort as a normal rite of passage, and although it might be common among new mothers, nothing about it is fucking normal.

Labor, delivery, and early motherhood create an emotional whirlpool and a complete reckoning on our bodies. It's the biggest transition a woman will ever go through in her life, but most women have no clue how hard it is on their bodies. Many new moms just don't realize that not only will they need help in taking care of their new baby, but also they're going to need help caring for themselves. Our newly postpartum bodies require time to recover, and we can't do that if we're cooking dinner, doing laundry, and staying up all night. A new mom needs the opportunity to heal so that she can have a solid foundation on which to build her new motherhood experience.

That might sound like a bunch of hippie babble, but really think about it. If you're depleted, overtired, underfed, and still recovering from a major medical procedure, don't you think you might struggle a bit more to bond with your baby? Won't breastfeeding feel that much more stressful? It's really easy to sob over feeling totally alone if you're left totally alone.

How is it that we don't know all this? It's not like every other woman before us had this easy, breezy time; it's just that most women have chosen not to share their experience and, therefore, many first-time moms don't have a real understanding of what's going to happen when they descend into new motherhood. They walk out of the hospital with a baby, a donut to sit on in the car, and a bag of diapers, with a nurse offering a feeble, "Good luck! Sleep when the baby sleeps!"

Uh, okay. Thanks? It's harder to adopt a dog than it is to leave the hospital with your baby. (I should know; I have two of each.)

Because it's not talked about, modern mothers don't plan for the type and amount of support they'll need because they don't fully grasp the seriousness and significance of this event.

Most women agonize over a birth plan to address every last detail, from whether they want drugs to who is allowed in the birthing room and the music that is playing at the time their child enters the world. We do all that work to prepare for a moment but don't create a plan for the days and weeks after.

To make matters worse, and for reasons beyond my understanding (and well beyond the scope of this book), social pressure has tricked new mothers into believing that how quickly they rebound from this postpartum period is an indicator of just how good they'll be at motherhood.

Having a baby isn't like getting a bit of dental work done. Regardless of how you deliver, a fully formed human being exits your body. That's crazy! If it takes us forty weeks to get ready to have the baby, why the hell do we expect to be back to our pre-baby selves—emotionally, mentally, and physically—before leaving the hospital? As I write, I'm five months postpartum with my second baby, and I still can't get my butt into my pre-pregnancy jeans. (As I edit, I'm eight months postpartum and, yep, still in my yoga pants.) This lends itself to a larger conversation about the expectations of women in modern culture, but that's for another time and place.

If you haven't heard it yet, let me be the first to tell you: you look fucking amazing, and I hope you feel amazing too, but, girl, don't you dare try to cook dinner the day you get home from the hospital . . . hell, don't cook dinner the first month! Don't worry if you miss a friend's birthday lunch or if you forgot to do the laundry; YOU JUST HAD A BABY! Go easy on yourself, Mama.

Give yourself time. Lots of time. I get it: you want to feel like yourself again. I did too, desperately, but you need to find other ways beyond pressuring yourself to perform at your pre-baby level. Indulge in the "lazies" as long as you can and as long as you have the support around you to accommodate it. Don't leave your bedroom for as long as possible! Watch movies on Netflix, and eat as much good food as you can. Allow yourself the time and space you need to rebound. You can't force Mother Nature, and there ain't no use trying.

And when you feel strong and ready, go for a walk or head to the coffeehouse by yourself for thirty minutes. Your baby won't suffer if you leave him or her with your mom or a friend for half an hour. Your baby *will* suffer if his or her mom is unhealthy, unhappy, and pushed past her natural limits. Happy mama, happy baby! Your child is an extension of you; for the first few weeks of life, your baby doesn't even know that he or she is a separate being. So, it goes without saying that if you are a bundle of nerves, your baby will be a bundle of nerves. If you're having an anxiety attack while breastfeeding, it's only natural to assume that your baby is feeling it too. Every new mom needs a chance to unplug, so it's important that new moms get comfortable handing their baby off to someone else for even just thirty minutes a day so they can shower, nap, watch an episode of *Friends,* or just sit alone in their room.

If for no other reason than because it is the best thing you can do for your kid, be good to yourself. I wasn't the first time around, and I really paid a price.

* * *

If the body trauma wasn't enough to challenge a postpartum woman, her hormones will happily make up the difference. After my daughter was born, I remember feeling so depleted, but I wasn't educated on what was happening to my body during recovery. I didn't realize how severe the hormone drop and nutrient depletion would be afterward and the havoc that it could wreak.

During pregnancy, the placenta produces levels of progesterone much higher than our body is used to (hello, mermaid hair!). When we deliver, the placenta is also expelled and our progesterone does a complete nosedive (dropping by 300 percent), leading to something called estrogen dominance, which is often the reason so many new mothers experience such symptoms as fatigue, anxiety, sadness—otherwise known as "baby blues."

Unlike postpartum depression and perinatal mood and anxiety disorders (which I discuss more in Chapter 10), baby blues is the body's reaction to the process of giving birth. As a result, it's treated as a temporary state that is expected to resolve within two weeks postpartum. But even with that knowledge, it still feels completely overwhelming to experience and it's not really necessary for women to wallow in those blues. Your body is rebalancing itself, and you need to make sure you are treating it with care, which means healthy food, plenty of water, lots of rest, and, for many, physical therapy and massage. Proper postpartum care and recovery can actually help new moms avoid experiencing baby blues.

So, how is it that I had zero idea about what my postpartum experience would look and feel like?

Because I didn't know the answer but wanted to give you expert advice and information, I reached out to talk with someone who did. Kimberly Johnson, cofounder of STREAM School for Postpartum Care and author of *The Fourth Trimester,* has made it her life's work to help women transition into motherhood. To hear her tell it, people just aren't educating themselves about childbirth. In fact, fewer women are prepping for childbirth now than in years past.

That sounded totally crazy to me, until I realized I was one of them. I didn't actually think to ask questions about what would be happening to me, my body, and my baby—and not a single one of my healthcare providers advised me otherwise.

Once again, I planned for the baby, not the experience of having the baby.

Apparently, I'm not the only one.

"I ask people, 'What's your postpartum plan?'" Johnson says, "and they say, 'my husband's taking ten days off work,' and I'm like, 'Yeah, and what's your postpartum plan?'"

Just as we need to spend our pregnancy preparing for the major shift in identity we undergo as women becoming mothers, I also believe we must prepare for our postpartum bodies and restoring our depleted resources.

"Think about it this way: a new mom has the same needs as a newborn—contact, loving touch, presence," she says. "You wouldn't leave a newborn alone for more than an hour and a half or two hours; and a new mom really needs that same kind of protection. A new mom needs a constant food source, rest, and a calm environment."

Because we're so trained to focus on bouncing back, we don't plan for the "lying-in" period that all new moms should be afforded. It's a time for bonding and for rest. How long this period traditionally lasts is specific to different cultures, but standard protocol requires *at least* two weeks: fourteen days doing nothing except sleeping, eating, and feeding your baby.

According to Johnson, Ayurveda—a system of alternative medicine—promotes the ideas of "forty-two days for forty-two years."

"How we're treated and the support we have in the first forty-two days postbirth is going to dictate how the next forty-two years of our life goes health-wise," she explains. "If we set ourselves up for the best care possible and view it as a necessity and not a luxury, then we can come out of that time healthier, more whole, and more prepared for the next steps."

However, instead of honoring that, many moms start competing with other new moms on who can bounce back quickest. We're deceiving our minds and our bodies by pretending that what we're experiencing is "normal." We use that label as a means of writing off all the kooky shit happening to our bodies and minds. If anything, we're setting ourselves up to fail: our families, our babies, and ourselves. No one wins when we don't honor the crazy journey our minds and bodies have just undergone. If anything, I believe that the stress this causes creates a more challenging transition for everyone involved.

Sure, maybe some celebrity fitness trainer put it on social media that she is back to her pre-pregnancy weight fourteen days after delivery and just cleaned out her garage, while breastfeeding and meal planning for the week, but tune out that noise, mamas. That is *not* the average woman's journey, so why even bother comparing yourself to it? Just do what I do: make passive-aggressive comments (totally healthy, right?). Tell yourself she's probably super unhappy or secretly hates her husband or is a space alien—none of which is true—just so you can feel a bit better about the large bowl of ice cream you're going to eat. Listen, I tell you later about how judging other women is not cool, but I think it's fair to say that if you have your pre-baby bod back in the first few weeks, don't share that shit with people. Good for you, and all, but aren't you winning enough? Do you have to rub my chin(s) in it?

So much of our postpartum experience depends on how we approach our postpartum recovery. Studies suggest that the level of postpartum care a mother receives has a direct and impactful correlation with her chances of developing a perinatal mood and anxiety disorder (including postpartum depression). It makes sense if you think about it. If we're resting and replenishing, being loved and cared for while recovering from pregnancy and delivery, as well as having both our needs and our child's needs cared for, then the lower the chances we'll spiral into that dark place when shit starts going sideways.

The best thing you can do for your new child in those early days of motherhood is to fill your own cup and focus on your recovery. So many of the challenges I faced as a new mom—and there were plenty—could have been lessened or avoided entirely if I had come out of surgery expecting to feel, look, and act like I went to battle for my baby, and not to look like I did pre-pregnancy. Unrealistic expectations allowed me to feel like I was a human trash bag when I failed to live up to an improbable standard, and from there everything else seemed to unravel. In reality, if I would have turned off the outside noise and focused on resting, I likely would have coped better with this incredible life event . . . and probably would have saved a lot of money on therapy.

TAKE FUCKING CARE OF YOURSELF, AND ALLOW OTHERS TO TAKE CARE OF YOU

A postpartum body is something to be honored; we're recovering from a trauma—a beautiful, welcome trauma, but a crazy experience all the same.

Whether you had your child vaginally, with or without medication, in a hospital, with a midwife, or via C-section, you probably weren't told how to properly care for your recovering body. Most doctors recommend that you rest for six weeks, wear a belly band, and sit on a donut (if needed). That's about it, which is *crazy*. Your body just went through the single most transformative event of your life, and you're told to "rest for six weeks."

When we tear our ACL, doctors suggest up to nine months of strict physical therapy. When delivering a baby tears apart our vaginas, doctors tell us to take some Tylenol and sit on a bag of frozen peas. Something about that seems a bit off.

Caring for our postpartum bodies and minds is personal and an essential every woman should indulge in. It's not always easy, and most likely you won't be able to do it all, but it's important that you partake in some self-care practices.

- **Allow yourself an extended rest period.**
  When my sister got home from the hospital after delivering my second nephew, she wrapped a belly band around her midsection, made a cheese board for visiting guests, and went to take her very large dog for a walk. I love her, but what the hell

was she thinking? Her body wasn't ready for any real activity. (Note: I recently questioned her about this series of events, and she remembers using the dog as an excuse to get out of the house; the reality of being a mother of two babies in diapers was sinking in.) During my own postpartum recovery, I couldn't properly process what was happening in my body because painkillers were masking a lot of the aches and pains. Even though a few days after delivery I felt well enough to walk around, I definitely should not have. Postpartum expert Johnson suggests employing her fifteen-day rule: "Five days in the bed, five days on the bed, and five days around the bed." Basically, you shouldn't be cruising the Target aisles ten days postpartum (but after ten weeks, it could be a total lifesaver). Moreover, Johnson suggests women take enough time predelivery to prepare. "Being in a courtroom on Friday and a hospital delivering a baby on Saturday doesn't give your nervous system an adequate chance to make the shift into what's required to birth a baby," says Johnson. You have to give yourself enough time to chill out before having the baby, which is hard because, if you're a working mom, you want to save as much time as you can for maternity leave. Yet, the quieter your mind and mental state before having the baby, the more productive your postpartum experience will be (think mood, breastfeeding, bonding).

- **Embrace warming practices.**
  Disclaimer: I live in California, which means I'm a crunchy coastal hippie who puts flaxseed in my smoothie (omega-3 fatty acids are essential, yo!). This sounds a little like voodoo witchcraft stuff, but the idea is that the postpartum body best responds to warm stimuli, so new moms need to surround themselves with all things *warm,* even if you had your baby in August in Chicago and you're desperate for an ice-cold milkshake. Think teas and spices—like cumin, cinnamon, ginger, and

coriander, which can promote postpartum recovery because they are rich sources of iron and loaded with antioxidants, fight inflammation, and support digestive health. Stock your fridge with bone broth too! Not only does it have collagen to help promote tissue repair, it's also very on trend right now. You can make it yourself or find it at a local natural foods store. Bonus: If you want people you know to think you're hip, post a photo of your bone broth on Instagram. People will be like, "This woman knows what's up!" Johnson also suggests keeping your body warm externally: socks, cozy blankets, heating pads, you name it! "The whole ice pack on the perineum thing is just the wrong direction," she says. It also sounds really painful, if you ask me. (Note: I have a few friends who *swore* by their ice pack.)

* **Say okay to vaginal steaming.**
Now that Chrissy Teigen made it socially acceptable, we can all adopt this practice into our postpartum care. It still feels creepy, though, right? I get it. Even the term itself, "vaginal steaming," feels a bit much. Ultimately, though, it makes sense to take care of your lady parts after pregnancy and childbirth, especially those of you who pushed human life out of your body via that specific region. Steaming is an extension of the warming practices, with the idea that steaming (warmth) is more effective for healing than ice. To hear Johnson tell it, it's also a more effective way to clean the area—versus the superglamorous squirt bottle—and it helps to close the cervix, increase blood flow, and encourage your organs to return to their optimal place. I don't know about you, but I'd really prefer my uterus doesn't fall out of my vagina (not that this will happen if you don't steam; I'm just putting it out there that I'd like mine to stay inside my body). For a reasonably low investment (about $100), you can have a steam chair and all the herbs you'd need, Johnson says. Sure, $100 is still $100 . . . and

a lot of money. But if you're one of those people who spent $40 on a wipes warmer—guilty!—a vaginal steam might be worth considering.

* **Request proper postpartum medical care.**
Here's the deal: medical care for women after childbirth is sort of a bummer. Our six-week checkup is basically an opportunity for doctors to clear us for sex and exercise (neither of which I really felt a lot like doing after only six weeks). In 2018, the American College of Obstetricians and Gynecologists released a report recommending that healthcare providers see postpartum women more frequently after childbirth. It's a great step forward, for sure, but it's likely still not enough. Mamas, you need to take your health care into your own hands. Not only does this mean asking your doctor for blood panels in the first few months postpartum, including a thyroid check, but also a referral to a pelvic floor therapist. The idea of women seeking physical therapy postpartum is only considered abnormal in the United States—in places like France and Holland, this is already routine. On top of body care, I think that most women would hugely benefit from checking in with a postpartum therapist or psychiatrist. Given the large number of women who suffer from perinatal mood and anxiety disorders after having a baby, it only makes sense! Honestly, I think it should be suggested to all new moms. Not only does it afford us a chance to get the hell out of the house, it also provides an environment where we can focus on ourselves and talk about how we feel. I love therapy, but, again, I live in LA: therapists are like a good dry cleaner—everyone has one.

* **It's not a good time to go vegan.**
As much as women might want to eat salads and drink smoothies to get back into their pre-baby form, this is not the right

time to do that, for so many reasons. For starters, these foods are hard to digest—for you and for your baby. Though kale and broccoli might help your figure, they're not going to do much for your milk supply. "You've got to have a lot of fat in your diet," Johnson says. "Like two tablespoons of butter at every meal." Additionally, try to incorporate healthy fats like avocado, coconut oil, and salmon as well as protein-rich food to help aid in tissue repair. Roasting a chicken nightly is probably out of the question (as it should be, girl, you just had a baby!), so stock up on protein shakes, nut butters, and turkey jerky.

* **Gather your mama tribe.**
I'm going to talk a lot about the importance of developing your new mama community in this book. I talked a bit about it in Chapter 2 but will explore it more in Chapter 6, because it's such a big deal that it requires its own chapter. As Johnson said earlier, new moms need the same things newborns need: physical support, comfort, food, and care. We need to look to our community and find the women who can "mother" us during this time. New moms shouldn't be alone, and, once again, ours is one of the few cultures that allows this. I get it: maybe you don't live near family, maybe your friends don't have kids, childcare is expensive, and maybe you're just used to doing it all yourself. But, girl, figure it out. (I say that with love.) Think of it as part of your pre-baby checklist: (1) Get a crib. (2) Buy diapers. (3) Find some mama support. Look online for resources in your community. Chances are your hospital or birthing center offers a postpartum support group or network. Ask friends to set up a meal train, and try to spread out any planned visits from family so you can make the most of the help. And as much as your mom or mother-in-law or crazy aunt might drive you up a wall, you can rest assured that

she loves your baby sufficiently to keep him or her alive long enough for you to shower or take a cat nap.

- **Slow the fuck down.**
I've said it a couple times now, but the most important thing a new mama can do is to allow herself the grace to recover at a normal pace—not a celebrity mom or Instagram mom pace. You *have* to ignore all the outside noise; it's not good for you and it's not good for your baby. A new mom is not supposed to be running errands after childbirth. Why? BECAUSE SHE JUST HAD A BABY! Acknowledging that it's a huge deal doesn't make you weak; it makes you strong enough and smart enough to know it as a life-altering experience. "It's the message across the board in everything I teach," Johnson says. "You want better sex? Slow down. You want a better postpartum experience? Slow down. You want to have better relationships? Slow down. You want to feel healthier? Slow down."

The bottom line is that women need to quit pretending that childbirth is just another thing we can "girl boss" our way through. You can't, and you shouldn't. What does a new mom gain by putting on the façade that she is bouncing back at record speed and that she can handle the baby, handle the house, and handle herself without any help? She's not doing anyone any favors by pressuring herself, and she's just furthering this narrative for other moms who think they need to do the same. Be lazy, be indulgent, and really try to relish those sweet first moments . . . because they don't last forever.

4 BUT IT LOOKS SO EASY ON INSTAGRAM

Seriously, how did she have time for a manicure? I glared at the screen, equal parts jealous, impressed, and horrified.

It seemed preposterous that anyone with a newborn could not only leave her home and have enough time to get her nails polished ruby red but also maintain it for more than a day. I looked again, searching for any glimpse of normalcy in this cropped square of perfection. The new mom sat on a made bed (red flag!), with her baby boy slumbering on her bent legs; she had the kind of thick, brunette hair that pulled up into an impressive movie-star-quality bun, and her small child was dressed in a white cashmere sweater set (that certainly had never seen a diaper blowout).

Was she wearing nonmaternity denim? I gasped. Her baby was, like, two weeks old! What was going on here?

I began to wonder: Was there a "Motherhood Perfected" filter on Instagram that I had somehow missed? I couldn't remember ever seeing it, but it had to be there. It's definitely not "Mayfair" or "Nashville." Maybe it's VSCO? I'm not 100 percent sure what that even means, but I've seen enough hashtags to know it's "a thing."

I gaped at this Goddess Mom, who seemed to be soaking in all the joys of early motherhood while seemingly avoiding all the pitfalls. Just a few days earlier, she posted a photo of herself wrapped in a chunky cable-knit cardigan while holding a coffee, again her hands manicured, this time a shade of ballet slipper pink, and impossibly moisturized.

So maybe she was just really good at painting her own nails, but was she not using medical-grade hand sanitizer? Sure, it dehydrates the skin to the point of scaling, but I wasn't going to risk spreading germs to my baby like this woman apparently was.

When I finally broke my iPhone trance long enough to survey my own reality, I saw that my life as a new mom looked nothing like the gorgeously shadowed little squares that I was thumbing through. I was more likely to be covered in urine than diva ring lighting, and my family room looked like I was one of the mole people living in an abandoned subway tunnel. My life was a fucking mess.

Let me take this opportunity to point out the giant dancing elephant in the room: many of you are probably reading this book because you discovered me on Instagram. And, yes, my photos often look like, wait for it, cropped squares of perfection. You're probably thinking, *Um, hi, hypocrite!* and you would be correct. In my efforts to connect with other new moms who felt lost and alone in early motherhood, I created a social media platform that allowed me to grab your attention before hitting you with the real-real. So, if you happen across my Instagram (@leslieannebruce), you might gravitate toward a picture of my son and me lying head-to-head on a perfectly made bed, only to find a caption that reads: "The isolation is real. Newborn land is tough. Roman is going through a growth spurt, so I constantly have a human head attached to my boob. Even with help, getting out of the house isn't easy. If I want to go somewhere at two p.m., I need to start planning at five a.m., and even then I don't always make it out. Also, I sliced my finger on a saranwrap box. I'm crushing the motherhood game, y'all!" As you keep reading this chapter, you'll discover that my issue isn't necessarily with the beautiful photos (who doesn't like pretty pictures?); it's with the Instamoms who pretend that those perfectly posed photographs are indicative of their actual daily life (spoiler alert: they're not).

Before I even ventured down the Social Media Mom rabbit hole as a new mother, I was already having a much harder time than I could have imagined: from baby blues and sleep deprivation to wildly engorged breasts and a searing pain across my midsection every time I walked up and down stairs. I didn't need the optic peer pressure of Instagram to cause me to further feel inadequate as a parent; the natural force of the reproductive experience was doing a fine job on its own.

And as for this woman, with her casually chic and airy aesthetic, she was really getting under my skin. Her life as a new mom appeared so effortless, and I wondered if that was how early motherhood should be. My little girl deserved an effortless, calm, casual mama too, but I was anything but. I desperately wanted to be like the woman in the photo—manicure and all—but I couldn't, so the next best thing was to hate her.

I bet her husband thinks she's boring.

Her baby isn't that cute.

She probably has hideous stretch marks.

I thought that telling myself that this woman was horrible in real life would make me feel better; it didn't. Shitting on someone else almost never makes anyone *really* feel better. This woman—who was assuredly in a happy marriage, who had an adorable child, and who most likely had not a single stretch mark—piqued my every insecurity, and, wow, did I hate feeling insecure. I hated that I evidently sucked at motherhood. I hated that I didn't look like the happy mama in the photo.

I also couldn't shake the feeling that it appeared to be entirely my own fault. As a mother, I couldn't find the time to have a photo-worthy new mom experience, which must have meant I was doing something wrong.

Let's be honest, though, this beautiful Instamama was not alone. There seemed to be an entire army of new moms living picture-perfect existences with their young children all over social media. They are the beautiful unicorn moms of Instagram.

Their feeds showcase one idyllic moment after another through cotton-candy filters and magic hour lighting. The new mothers, with impossibly long eyelashes, always look so serene as they breastfeed their cherubic newborns (whose perfectly shaped heads show zero signs of labor). They resemble something of a modern "Madonna and Child," nestled into a swirl of crisp, clean sheets. Or those rage-inducing newborn shoots in which a perfectly photoshopped infant is sleeping with his or her bobbly head propped up by two tiny fists, like this infant just bellied up to a bar and fell asleep. (I'm 100 percent guilty of staging a shoot like this and slapping it on my holiday cards, only mine included a hot pink shag rug and a stack of black-and-white-striped tea cups.)

IN DEFENSE OF NEWBORN PHOTOS

Despite being somewhat ridiculous, many new moms succumb to newborn photo shoot mania. I'm as guilty as the next mama and, yes, they 100 percent pander to the parts of our psyche that want to project the appearance that everything is picturesque in newborn land: our sweet babies sleeping peacefully in baskets or on tiny wrought-iron beds or on top of a stack of pancakes . . . you know, normal shit.

Here's the thing: taking newborn photos was actually a small opportunity for me to feel good about my new postpartum identity and, truthfully, feel like one of those beautiful Instamamas (if only for a day). The photographer is usually—and should be—well trained in handling newborns, which frees up our hands for a bit. I used the time to wash and style my hair and put on some makeup.

The photographer's job is also to make a new mother look and feel her best in the photos, and it's nice to feel doted on. Baby photo shoots are an expense, that's for sure, but taking newborn photos can be a nice reprieve from the daily grind, and, at the end of it, you have these beautiful photos that you can hand out as holiday or birthday gifts to family members for *at least* a year.

* * *

Although most rational humans can recognize the "Instamom phenomenon" for what it is (an epidemic that promotes an overglamorized version of motherhood and captures a moment in time, not real life), in the hormonal blur of sleepless nights, I couldn't see the forest for the trees. Never once did I look at one of those photos and think, "Yep. Same." Mostly, I just thought about how it seemed like every other woman was having an easier, more photo-worthy experience than I was. Scrolling through these alternate realities often caused me to feel devalued, anxious, and unsuccessful. For some reason, none of these women ever seemed to suffer from clogged milk ducts or chapped nipples. I couldn't understand why their babies never, ever had gas or how these moms were already back in their size 4 dresses when their kids were, like, forty-five minutes old.

I had been successfully "Instashamed," which caused me to become bitter and jealous, so I would make snide comments about how they were probably the type who did yoga the day they delivered and had packed "vegan-friendly" snack options for the hospital. I'd pass judgment on these women for being the type of mothers who made their own nut milk while I secretly wished to be the type of mother who made her own nut milk.

Eventually, my snark and criticism subsided and forced me to reflect (as they always do), and I actually began blaming myself for our subpar existence: I never took my newborn on sunset beachside strolls, and I never wore floppy hats or lined my forearm with gold bangles. I never once wandered into a field at dusk wearing a crown of lavender only to place my baby in the bottom drawer of an odd, but conveniently placed antique French dresser. And when was the last time my husband, my newborn, and I stumbled upon a distressed velvet sofa in a random back alley? Never! Why did other moms seem to have all the luck?

Even the "I'm gonna keep it real" photos seemed like a fucking fantasy: a bonnet-adorned baby sound asleep in an artisan Moses basket while the caption halfheartedly laments the challenges of new motherhood. (While we're on the topic, can we discuss when the hell bonnets became trendy again? Did I miss the memo?) Never does the mom say in her caption, "Wow, if I have to sterilize one more breast pump part, I might actually stick my head in the motherfucking oven." No, no, no . . . it's always something more like, "At least one of us can nap today." Insert crazy-face emoji here. Don't tell me how exhausted you are; tell me that you've pissed through an adult diaper and you have vomit in your hair. I don't need your barely there complaints to only further make myself feel like shit because I have actual, normal struggles.

Even those "look at how crazy my life is—more wine, please!" mamas came across as semi-disingenuous. They hid behind hyperbole and sensationalized moments of chaos. They smeared black mascara under their eyes ("do it for the 'gram!"), snapped pictures of themselves making an "OMG!" face after a perfectly prop-styled smoothie explosion in their kitchen, after which they would whip up nifty little songs about how their toddler tried to flush toys down the toilet—sung to the tune of the latest Beyoncé single—and uploaded it to YouTube. The overly dramatized moments were often just as duplicitous as the overly perfect moments. Just once, why didn't one of these people say: "My baby just hit me in the face, my dog just peed on the couch, I picked up my water bottle by the lid I forgot to screw on, and I spent the morning crying because none of my pants fit. I don't like my kid, I don't like my dog, I don't like myself, and I don't like my closet."

To see it playing out on Instagram, I was the only one truly stressed, and that was perhaps the worst feeling of all. Sure, I should've just tuned it out altogether, but that's much easier said than done. During those early days, when moms barely have time to leave the house, we often use social media as a barometer of our experience. This is when we most need a reality check, but many of us are unable to rise above the weeds to recognize this logic.

Social media caused me to question everything. Not only did these Instamoms have enough time, and energy, to really enjoy this new experience, but they also seemed to be successfully managing their homes, their babies, and themselves. I couldn't understand how that was possible. Everything around me appeared to be recently struck by a Category 5 hurricane. It was an impossible battle that I was clearly losing.

I'd failed at things before in my life, but I was the only person to suffer those consequences. When it came to being a mom, I was not only disappointing myself but also letting down my sweet girl, who deserved better than I felt I could give her. Whatever the price, she paid it right alongside me, and that was a devastating blow to consider. All of my planning and prepping couldn't compensate for the one thing I wanted more than anything: to be a really awesome mom for Tallulah. I really started to believe that I was blowing it.

Unbeknownst to me at the time, my version of reality was *not* abnormal. What was abnormal was the hyperproduced photos of camera-ready mamas and their angelic newborns that I kept seeing. These images prey on our every vulnerability, which can be especially hard for new and first-time mamas.

I'm not breaking any news here, but Instagram can cause anxiety in users because it cultivates a culture of FOMO (fear of missing out). Users begin to feel "less than" about their own experience when comparing themselves to others on the platform. Before having my daughter, I was as guilty as the next user for subscribing to this idea (apparently, I used to have an adventurous, interesting life). In recent years, that anxiety has been linked to the rise in teen suicide (nearly 400 percent), for one, meaning this shit can seriously be dangerous if not properly understood—and it's also the reason my daughter isn't getting a phone until she's forty-five.

Here's where I'm gonna turn into a bit of a Silicon Valley geek for a minute. Though I don't want to bog us down with weird tech jargon like "content marketing" and "embedding," I do think that understanding the backstory can help mamas more easily come to terms with their own realities and forgive themselves for not having a picture-perfect life.

In the beginning, many of us viewed Instagram as a digital photobook that enabled us to share photos with friends and family. I mean, I don't know about you, but I've never thumbed through a baby book, electronic or otherwise, and seen a collection of screaming newborn photos. But Instagram has become, as we all know, so much more than that. Over time, it has evolved into this living, breathing community that people turn to for real-time entertainment, inspiration, news, and support while it also became an overwhelmingly powerful platform for brands and "influencers" (seemingly average people who have developed a social media following based on their unique voice, photography, and/or expertise within a particular space).

The "mama influencer" is one of these many verticals (a space that, as I explained earlier, I am now guilty of being in myself) across all social media. Within this space, inadvertently a subculture of peer pressure developed, where finding success as a new mother and an appreciation for this new role were best represented through thoughtfully produced photos (whether intended to be beautiful and syrupy or outlandishly chaotic and humorous). What users see is the end result (the photo) and not the reality that many "mama influencer" accounts use professional photographers, prop stylists, and hair and makeup teams. And before the #ad and #sponsored hashtags were required to appear by law, users didn't realize that some of these influencers were paid to produce this content (I guess we can thank the Fyre Festival for something!). It really is a job for some people. And that right there is the rub: most people on Instagram don't know all this!

None of this is surprising because it's just the "motherhood" flavor of what social media does as a whole: panders to that sense of FOMO. My concern is that putting polished images on a pedestal and embracing them as reality (especially when it's becoming easier and easier to manipulate photos) creates unrealistic expectations for other new moms and moms-to-be. When your core demographic is overworked, overtired, and overstressed mamas, it feels less like FOMO and more like failure.

Over the course of creating my own motherhood brand, I have built a substantial social media platform, and, as I explained earlier, I often post carefully curated and stylized photos of my daughter, my home, and myself that hopefully attracts the attention of users. So, aren't I guilty of feeding the very beast I just named?

Great point. The answer is yes . . . and no. Social media isn't going anywhere anytime soon, and it is a way to connect with moms who need support, humor, and community. Here's the thing: people don't always want to engage with photos that aren't agreeable to look at, so, in order to reach as many new mamas as I can, I, too, post pretty images that mamas hopefully want to click on. But capturing these photos isn't an effortless part of my day; it calls for early morning glam squads, professional photographers, countless hours on Etsy searching for snarky mommy and me T-shirts, days of prep, and so on.

But all of that is just to get your attention, because once you're there, my intent is to offer honest and raw conversation about what goes on behind the photo and what is really happening in my motherhood journey. I talk about my struggle with postpartum anxiety and how isolated I felt in the early days after my son was born. I use video to offer mamas weekly postpartum updates or to discuss my hormone-induced confrontation with an old guy at the park who was yelling at children for "vandalizing public property" (aka using chalk on the sidewalk).

Yes, the photos I post often are pretty and professionally shot, but that doesn't mean my daughter didn't scream because I forced her to wear the Rainbow Brite costume I wore as a child or because she had her first taste of ice cream and decided she HATED ice cream (whose child is she?). If I post a beautiful photo of my daughter in some minimalist Scandinavian chair in my living room, I acknowledge that I have dirty breakfast dishes sitting in the sink, that I pushed a basket of gross-looking dog toys out of the frame, and that though my kids look adorable, I am wearing my husband's old high school T-shirt and no pants. I try to balance as much as I can, but my primary goal is always to remind people that the photo I post is *just a photo*.

I think we could all stand to be a bit more honest about what we're launching into the world. Our goal should be to build a community of support and realism that acknowledges many roads lead to Rome and that we're all just trying to be the best mamas and women we can be. Motherhood is as varied and diverse as each of the women who embark on the journey. I have amazing moments and difficult moments; good days and bad days. It's real life.

As Instagram evolves, we have to evolve with it. I'm not suggesting we share only photos of our crying babies or the breast milk–stained T-shirt we've been wearing for three days. My advice for new mamas is to take all those beautiful Instamom photos with a grain of salt, because a carefully cropped square leaves the rest of a person's reality out of the frame.

Who knows, maybe if we all started accepting that it's okay to be less than perfect, that would become the new normal, not just on social media but in our communities as well. We need to replace mom shaming with mom cheering, mom blaming with mom accepting, and mom competing with mom loving.

But, until that happens, maybe keep a velvet-tufted sofa in your garage on the off chance you're having a good hair day and can snap a pic of your baby on it, and every once in a while treat yourself to a ruby-red manicure.

5

THINGS MIGHT SUCK FOR A WHILE

I dropped my six-week-old.

I cringe even now, four years later, seeing those words in black and white. I dropped my beautiful baby girl onto her crib mattress, much more carelessly than I like to admit. It happened so quickly that I can't be certain at what point my fingers released her, but I remember it startling her enough that she began to wail. I hadn't slept more than three hours straight since before she was born, I was roughly twenty-four hours away from embarking on a really fun new adventure called mastitis, and I believe now that I was suffering from a degree of postpartum depression.

While those three things are absolutely true, they are also excuses I'm making because I feel wildly ashamed knowing that people are going to read this.

But I shouldn't, and that's the point. I dropped my precious Tallulah, my heart outside my body, because I was losing my mind.

I spent those early days alone in my home with a young child who rarely slept while my husband was at work. My mother had spent the first four weeks in and out of Los Angeles to help me during the days, and I knew I was lucky for having that, but she was long gone. Most of my friends had already come through the revolving door for their obligatory meet-and-greet and had since returned to their lives as well. I felt as if the world kept moving forward while I was stuck in some version of mom life purgatory.

My every waking minute was devoted to my beautiful little girl, who demanded all of my attention as I tried, hopelessly, to read her mind and meet her needs while I was myself recovering from an abdominal surgery during which a small person was pulled from my body. After any major surgery, a person is instructed to rest as much as possible and is forbidden from engaging in anything strenuous or stressful. After my C-section, I spent a mere twelve hours in bed before the nurse had me walking the maternity ward floor. Three days later, I was sent back home with an actual human being to care for.

I was teetering on the brink of insanity because I experienced sleep deprivation so severe it could've broken most hardened criminals—which explains why it's often used as a form of torture. Night after night, I spent hours trying to pacify a newborn who routinely wailed for no apparent reason.

Regardless of how little or how much she slept the night before, we woke up for the day by five a.m., but if I managed to get us out of the bedroom before eleven, that was a major cause for celebration. Looking back now, I can't be certain where those hours went; it was as if I had fallen into some newborn time warp. We woke up, fed, burped, and changed (her, not me). I rocked her back to sleep, which took anywhere from ten minutes to an hour (if she slept at all), before gently placing her in the bassinet, silently willing her to stay asleep during the transition. It was like handling a live grenade: slowly, cautiously, and with extreme precision.

If her eyes stayed shut (which they rarely did), I then needed to decide: Do I pump or shower? Shower or pee? Should I pee or eat? What order should I do them in? She would either sleep for fifteen minutes or fifty, so it was a complete coin toss. I could feasibly shower, pee, and eat at the same time, but if I were to pump, I might actually be able to leave the house that evening to get to the store, go for a walk, or cry by myself in the car.

But what if I pumped for fifteen minutes and then she woke up crying? I would have no milk left in my boobs to feed her, so I'd have to give her the bottle I just pumped, and then have nothing at all to show for all that "free time" I had: no shower, no bathroom relief, no full belly, and no promise of a future escape. (You can see just how quickly the "crazy" starts to kick in.)

And it's not like I could go for a drive or run a quick errand. Even if she didn't loathe her car seat (which she did), I rarely managed to get out of my pajamas or brush my hair. If we did happen to go somewhere, I had a thirty-pound diaper bag to tote along, complete with nipple shields and boob cream because breastfeeding had done some considerable, and permanent, damage.

I didn't recognize myself anymore, figuratively and literally (the hormone drop-off was swift and fierce). Everyone around me said that the first three months were going to be a challenge, but I was convinced that the arbitrary twelve-week timeline wouldn't apply to me. She and I were stuck together in our version of mommy jail for the foreseeable future, and the fact that I resented this blessed new life made me feel a million times worse. I decided I just wasn't built for motherhood.

It wasn't Tallulah's fault. She was a baby, and she was just doing what all babies do. The blame rested on my shoulders. My poor little girl needed a better mama than I thought I could be. Social media was already this blaring reminder of how motherhood *should* look; unfortunately for my daughter, she had just drawn the short straw in the new mom lottery.

You know how sometimes you just need a good cry? I *needed* a really good cry, but didn't have the energy or the time to dissolve into the mental breakdown I rightly deserved, because my beautiful little girl depended on me for every single facet of her young existence.

So, in a moment of true helplessness and absolute hysteria, I dropped my sweet baby girl into her crib. In retrospect it was less dramatic than it felt at the time, but that said, I now understand how women who suffer from a postpartum mood disorder can go to a dark place. At the time, I told myself it was just baby blues, but I don't believe that anymore. She was already six weeks, and the baby blues usually come and go within two. There was a larger issue happening; I just wasn't of sound enough mind to recognize it.

Let me set the record straight: I knew well enough to never actually harm my daughter, and I did not ever have the impulse or desire to, but I was hysterical enough to be pretty cavalier.

And while we're being honest, I also ripped her closet doors off the tracks with an unnatural strength and let out a guttural scream that arose from deep within.

Shit was getting weird.

I used to be powerful, collected, and engaged. I was a successful career woman who relaunched brands, who helped author *New York Times* best-selling books, and who had grown men and women twice her age answering to her, but despite every effort, I couldn't get my child to stop crying.

"Why doesn't she ever just stop!?" I growled at my husband, who had been standing behind me, blurry-eyed, confused, and then alarmed. Tallulah was crying at a pitch surely only dogs and new mothers could hear. A pull inside me urged me to pick her up, hold her tight, and immediately repent, but it was too late. I had stuck my flag in the ground and needed him to see how close to the edge I was tottering. Somewhere in my subconscious I knew that his presence secured our safety, hers and mine.

I stormed out of her nursery and headed to the kitchen, for what, I'm not sure. I opened the fridge and froze. In front of me was a cardboard pizza box crammed onto a shelf at, roughly, a twenty-five-degree angle. I knew that there were only two pieces of pizza left, so why was the entire box in my damn fridge? What was so difficult about putting the remaining slices in Tupperware or a Ziploc? Instead, my husband had shoved the entire fucking box into the refrigerator, leaving jam jars and soda cans wobbling on their edges, threatening to come tumbling out.

I looked at that giant, near-empty box and wondered whether he was expecting me to properly put away the remaining pizza. Why would he take the time to do it when he knew I would just eventually do it myself? I'd take it out, place the slices in a container, and take the box out to the recycling bin, like I had in the past.

But this wasn't the past. There was a baby here now who required all of my attention. I didn't have time for pizza boxes! If I told my husband to put away the leftover pizza like a normal human and take the box outside, I would inadvertently become the "nagging" wife every woman (and man) fears. If I did nothing and said nothing, I would become resentful. The box would spend the next few days on that shelf and eventually something would tip over and spill or shatter across the floor.

If that box knocks over my breast milk, I thought threateningly, readying myself for a brawl. Four ounces of breast milk equated to about ninety minutes of freedom. How could anyone be so careless with someone's freedom? Where was my soapbox? This was my Norma Rae moment! (That reference is most likely too old for many of you, but google it. Trust me.)

Whatever the casualty, I would definitely be the one burdened with the aftermath. Did he actually think I had time to deal with this shit right now? When? In between feedings while I scrubbed breast pump parts, did laundry, and fed the dogs? I barely had time to pee, but I was now somehow charged with teaching my adult husband to develop common fucking sense. (Upon reading this, my husband noted that he almost exclusively feeds the dogs nowadays. Someone should probably give him a trophy.)

Either way, this giant fucking pizza box was now my cross to bear.

To be fair, I knew I was snapping, but I didn't know how to avoid it. I needed to get out of there; I needed to escape my life. I was psychoanalyzing a pizza box! But I couldn't go anywhere; I was shackled to the house for as long as I was breastfeeding. I was a prisoner of my own device, which had me thinking about the Eagles and how I would cut off my arm to go to a concert . . . any concert. Give me a suburban Aerosmith cover band. Anything! I just needed a break!

"Shhhh, baby girl," I heard my husband whisper. "You're okay . . . it's okay."

I looked at the monitor and saw him gently rocking our beautiful, tiny baby. She was wide awake but momentarily calm, and that's when it washed over me, a guilt so horrible that I don't think it will ever leave me. There he was, comforting my sweet, innocent, perfect little girl. My daughter. My best friend. The person I love beyond all measure, and who I would give my life to protect. She was my reason for being, and, unbeknownst to me at the time, I would work every single day of my life to create for her a happy, healthy life and would willingly sacrifice myself for her every single day. This was the little girl who would one day crawl into my bed during a thunderstorm and ask me to kiss the boo-boo on her knee. This is the little girl who would sing Garth Brooks at the top of her lungs while I questioned my husband as to why he was letting her listen to "Much Too Young to Feel This Damn Old." This is the brave little girl who would get up onstage, at just two years old, to dance in front of two hundred people to a *Moana* song, and I would sob because I never experienced a pride and adoration so profound.

In that moment, staring at the baby monitor, I hated myself. I was a monster.

Leaving the fridge door still wide open as the pizza box clung for dear life, I ran back to the nursery. My husband was placing her down in her bassinet, and he looked back over his shoulder at me.

"Babe, I think you need to take a break," he said firmly. (Where was that logic ten minutes earlier?)

But I couldn't walk away right now. I needed to make it up to her; I was her mother. I needed to tell her I was sorry and that I was going to do better. I'd try harder. I'd be the mother she deserved.

"I just . . ." I said, the tears pouring down my face, but I found myself incapable of choking out any comprehensible words.

He walked toward me, and I took a few steps back. By the time I realized what he was doing, his large frame already occupied most of the doorway.

Holy shit, I thought. He was trying to protect her . . . from me. With a sudden sense of primal urgency, I tried to push past him, but he blocked me with his arms.

"You can't come in here right now," he said, keeping his voice steady, even though he was visibly upset.

"What are you saying?" My voice was cracking.

"You need to calm down."

Most men know that telling a woman to "calm down" doesn't usually elicit the response they're hoping for. That said, I would seriously advise against saying it to a six-week-postpartum woman.

My throat trembled with the shriek I wanted so desperately to release, but even at the exact moment of my own mental break, I knew better than to disrupt the momentary quiet. I ran upstairs and locked myself in the bathroom, where I sobbed and hyperventilated until I threw up. I wrapped my hair around my fingers and began tugging as hard as I could.

I didn't even know myself anymore. I had never tried to inflict self-harm before, but, in this moment, I desperately wanted to claw out of my own skin. I felt this pain so deeply, so acutely. I needed any distraction to pull me from this moment. But it was so much more than this moment, than my stellar parenting performance minutes earlier . . . it was so much more.

It was weeks upon weeks of frustration, exhaustion, and anxiety. Motherhood was so much harder than I ever imagined, and my postpartum self couldn't manage it all.

Despite what felt like my very best efforts, I just couldn't do it. My mother had done it, and her mother had done it with twins and at just nineteen years old! I couldn't make sense of my own struggle. I had managed to write a book in less than three months while overseeing our entire home renovation. I completed an eighteen-month graduate program in twelve. I even managed to sneak into Puff Daddy's exclusive VMA after-party in 2007. Yet, I couldn't figure out life with my baby.

To add insult to injury, I really adored my sweet little girl, but I felt like I was completely dropping the ball. It was so soul-crushing as to cause an otherwise sane woman to drop her child before pulling out her own hair. I didn't know how to do this.

I'm not sure how long I lay on the bathroom floor before I fell asleep, but about two hours later I was gently nudged awake by my husband with breasts the size of watermelons (me, not him) and a headache the size of Texas. It was nearly six in the morning and Tallulah was hungry. My husband apologized for not moving me to the bed, telling me that he thought it was more important to let me sleep. I went to the kitchen to search for a nipple shield and to grab myself a bottle of water.

The pizza box still taunted me from the fridge, but I ignored it. I would deal with that shit later. I would deal with my shit later. My priority now was my baby. I would make it up to her. I would get up, start over, and try again. And I would do it every day until I could become a mama my baby deserved.

SHIT YOU SHOULD KNOW: A LIST OF THINGS YOU MIGHT CRY OVER

» You tried on your pre-pregnancy jeans.

» Your husband did not listen to you.

» Your husband actually listened to you.

» Your baby will start school . . . in three years.

» You forgot your phone number.

» You can't pee alone.

» You peed your pants.

» The baby woke up before you could finish an episode of *Game of Thrones*.

» You went to get a string cheese from the fridge and realized you didn't buy string cheese.

» The baby kept you up all night. Then the next night, the baby sleeps through the night and you cry because "he doesn't need me anymore!"

» You told your husband not to touch you, so he doesn't touch you.

» The news.

» Any Pampers, Johnson & Johnson, or Shelter Pet commercial.

» Your food delivery got canceled.

» Nipple blisters.

» Nipple scabs.

» Nipple size.

» Nipples.

» Someone asked you when you're due.

» You told your friends you couldn't go to lunch, and they went without you.

» You forgot what "eyelashes" are called.

» Your baby has a rash, and you googled it . . .

- *The Bachelor*.
- There are no sterilized bottles.
- Your husband ate your last lactation cookie.
- You picked up the wrong mobile order at Starbucks.
- Your mom asked you to make her a sandwich. ("I don't care about your damn sandwich, Patricia!")
- Your bra gives you a uni-boob.
- You forgot to wash the conditioner out of your hair.
- Your mother-in-law cut the baby's nails too short.
- Your baby listened to his first Bruce Springsteen song . . . and you're from New Jersey.
- Someone ate your Oreos.
- Because banana pudding is so good.
- You're washing pump parts . . . again.
- Someone offered you a seat on the subway or bus.
- You forgot your paperwork for the DMV, but they let you slide, so now your driver's license picture is a photo of you crying. So you cry again.
- The bed wasn't made correctly.
- Baby clothes that no longer fit.

* * *

OKAY, SO THAT WAS HEAVY—and it wasn't easy for me to share. But the more women I connect with and talk to, the more I realize that my experience wasn't really rare. At the time, I just didn't know any better or any different; I thought I was all alone in my world of chaos and tears.

Psychologists suggest that properly "gaslighting" an individual takes a considerable amount of time. The perpetrator shouldn't expect to accomplish such a feat in a matter of weeks; gaslighting is a long game. The most effective attempts at driving a person clinically insane take place over the course of months, even years.

I wish someone would have shared that with my daughter. Almost all parents believe that their child is somehow advanced—and I was no exception. When it came to sending her mama mad, my baby girl had *talent*.

Throughout my pregnancy and during those early months, many people suggested I read *Happiest Baby on the Block* by Dr. Harvey Karp. Seemingly countless new moms consider his prescriptive tome the definitive work on caring for small humans during their first twelve weeks of life. His methods not only are proven to be effective through both real-world application and centuries of historical research but also have a foundation in actual science. But there's a caveat: the new parent must be level-headed and of sound mind to apply these techniques in modern culture.

Know this: once you have a baby, you're going to go bat-shit crazy. And that's what Karp manages, in my opinion, to gloss right over.

Hopeful and dismally optimistic new moms everywhere (myself included) read Karp's book, highlight a few paragraphs, and come to the same conclusion: well, that doesn't sound too terrible.

With nonchalant logic and irrational reason, Karp explains that surviving a child's infancy is simple—enjoyable, even—as long as new parents can master the five S's: swaddle, side, suck, shush, and swing. The reason being that in "the fourth trimester" of life, infants are most content when the parent can re-create the environment they experienced in the womb. Through the course of evolution, as human brains developed, our heads got larger, and the fetus needed to evacuate the womb earlier to make it through the birth canal because our vaginas literally can't get any larger. (Numerous studies and much research disputes this claim, which is the basis of Karp's entire theory, but I'll let you feel that one out on your own.)

In his *Happiest Baby* DVD (yes, I even watched the DVD), Karp strolls into the homes of new moms with washed hair and fresh mascara (a huge red flag), and within a matter of minutes, he has their fussy little bundle lulled into a soft and restful slumber by implementing his methods of soothing.

What the DVD doesn't show is what happens when you stop. Let's say you're shushing and swinging your fussy baby, who's swaddled and sucking while laying on her side, and she finally falls asleep. In that fleeting moment of peace, you place her gently into her bassinet so you can finally brush your teeth and put on deodorant for the first time in days. But as soon as the baby's head hits the cool mattress, she loses her mind. At least, that's what mine did.

Sure, Dr. Karp will admit that it does take practice, but rest assured: if your child isn't responding to the combination of these five techniques, it's not the child's fault—you're just doing it wrong. So keep trying. Again. And again. And again. If, like me, you've been blessed with a highly sensitive baby, the only way to successfully implement these techniques is to spend twelve weeks in a dark room sitting on an exercise ball bouncing and shushing your swaddled baby twenty-four hours a day, seven days a week . . . nonstop. Literally. You can't stop. It's not only unrealistic, it's absolutely absurd.

Although my daughter definitely fell on the "fussier" side when it came to newborns, she wasn't really the driving force behind my meltdown. Unbeknownst to me, my maddened state actually had much more to do with my mental and physical health; those challenging newborn moments didn't help, of course.

For the first few weeks, the initial shock of motherhood was intense, and the hormone imbalance caused me to feel anything from anxious and sad to hyper and manically happy; by week four or five, Tallulah's digestive tract was at the height of bacteria production, making her much fussier than normal (which is apparently a very normal newborn stage that I was just completely unaware of); and I was just so fucking tired. She and I were in the middle of a 9.0 earthquake, and I was so busy clinging on for dear life that I couldn't recognize it for what it was: temporary. I just saw my own failure, and a sweet baby who I so desperately wanted to be better for.

According to the National Institute of Mental Health, 80 percent of all new mothers experience "the baby blues" (which we'll dive into in Chapter 10), which typically last for one to two weeks, and a further 20 percent of those blue postpartum mothers actually suffer from a deeper condition, a perinatal mood or anxiety disorder (which could include postpartum depression). Even if you happen to be one of the lucky 20 percent who doesn't experience any type of negative mood, all new mamas experience a hormone nosedive; our bodies just all react differently to it. I wasn't aware of these statistics until long after the fog of newborn land had dissipated, and literally nothing and no one around me at the time gave any indication this was the case for so many women.

Our nutrient levels are starved from giving so much to our children (a statement that is far too layered to fully explore right now) during labor and delivery, and during lactation for those who choose to breastfeed. This has become such common knowledge that an entire market of niche products is geared toward postpartum women; just ask Gwyneth Paltrow, who peddles her new mother supplement packets—$90 for a month's supply—that promise to restore all that was diminished. You think that's over the top? Thanks to Kim Kardashian, an entire subculture of women are determined to eat their own placentas to replenish these lost nutrients.

There's still a lot of debate on this specific topic, so I'm not sure where I land. Though I'd much prefer not to, if there was a chance that popping a couple of placenta pills could save me from completely losing my shit, I'd probably give it a try. That being said, a study on the topic published in the *American Journal of Obstetrics and Gynecology* recently found that eating your own placenta may not actually do anything to reduce your risk of postpartum depression or hormone imbalance. I'm not gonna lie: if I blended my placenta into a smoothie and drank it only to later find it did nothing for my benefit, I would be *pissed*! But even if it is just a placebo effect (and I'm not saying that it is), and it works for you . . . then so be it. Get down with that placenta lasagna, girl. No judgment here!

All this doesn't even take into consideration the effects of sleep deprivation on a new mother and how it is directly correlated with the increased risk of developing perinatal mood and anxiety disorders. Or the fact that after a month or two at home with an infant, the burst of newborn excitement begins to fade, and women start to suffer with a gutting loss of self as they transition into this new role that has taken priority in life.

With all this physiological and mental chaos going on in our new mom bods, it makes perfect sense why so many of us struggle in those few first months of becoming mothers. As a rational, relatively rested woman, I can now understand this, but during that period of time, I was too consumed in the day-to-day of my own little world to see it.

The fourth trimester is fucking insane. It feels a little distasteful to compare life with a newborn to life in a war zone, but, for a new mother, the comparison may not be that far off base. Beginning when you bring your baby home from the hospital, life as you once knew it is over and every day presents its own set of challenges. Whether it's your hormones, your body, your baby, your exhaustion, your mental health, your husband, or your general hygiene, a new mom never knows what curveball she'll get thrown next.

To properly prepare for this transition, new moms need to start planning the day they find out they're pregnant. As discussed in Chapters 2 and 3, modern moms don't often take the time to prepare their bodies and their minds for this postpartum period because how the hell are they supposed to know? No one fucking talks about it!

Although there isn't much you can do to counterbalance the aftermath of pregnancy and childbirth once you're home, sometimes the comfort is simply in the knowing.

But that doesn't mean you should wallow in it. New moms need to recognize how fucking crazy all of this is, and, most importantly, they need to cut themselves some slack! In those early postpartum weeks, I wanted to have it all, be it all, and do it all, but I couldn't. That's when everything started to unravel. When it felt like my world was crumbling around me, the last thing I felt inclined to do was prioritize my needs, but that's exactly what I needed.

A BIT OF NEW MOM LIFE COACHING

I can tell you to go easy on yourself only so many times before you're sick of hearing it from me, so I called in backup. Heidi Stevens is a soulful business coach and spiritual psychologist (again, I live in California; this is the shit we do), mother of two, and one of the most calming spirits I have ever known. She offers these words of support:

> New motherhood is not the time for goal setting or planning; it's about giving yourself the permission to not get anything done besides keeping yourself and your baby alive, and filling your own tank the best way you know how. For one woman, that might be taking a shower, doing her hair, and making the bed. For another woman that might mean looking like a hot mess, lying on the couch all day, and cluster feeding. You are keeping another being alive; give yourself the gift of grace. Tell yourself: I have everything I need in this moment. I am safe. My baby is safe. I am healthy. My baby is healthy. I'm going through the biggest transition in my entire life, and I'm going to get on the other side.

The most restorative things new moms can do for themselves is indulge in whatever "me time" they can manage to spare, even if it feels inconvenient or stressful, and engage with other mothers. At no point in human history were new mothers left alone to handle this transition, and it is absolutely critical that all new mothers find time to give unto themselves. Keep in mind that this is all relative: a new mother won't have time for a hair appointment, a yoga class, and lunch with her friends before tucking into answering emails, but she is capable of taking anywhere from fifteen to sixty minutes a day to focus on her own well-being. That could mean sitting alone in your bedroom to close your eyes and breathe, or that could mean being willing to open up to another mama about your struggles. Often, just knowing that other women have had similar experiences can be some serious chicken soup for the soul. It can make this new chapter feel a lot less lonely.

In those early days, I was blessed with a husband and a nearby mom, and I still struggled to find the time, so I can't even begin to imagine how impossible it may feel for a single mom or a stay-at-home mom with three kids. But, ladies, you must carve out some small moments of calm for yourselves, whether that means calling on friends, neighbors, or people in your motherhood community. Maybe you can't figure it out every day, but every so often you *have* to find the time. It will serve your family as much as it serves you, because small respites can help save a new mom from the insanity and allow her some much-needed perspective before she goes apeshit over a pizza box.

And, in case you were wondering, I took it out to recycling.

TIPS FOR PRACTICAL SELF-CARE (THAT YOU CAN ACTUALLY MANAGE TO DO)

» Take a solo trip to Target or Costco. You will be amazed how cathartic it is to be alone in a store.

» Don't skip the shower. Just about every new mom I talk to says she feels her best when she has time to rinse off. It's a surprisingly satisfying daily milestone.

» Drink your coffee while it's hot. This can be tricky, because mornings can be really busy, but if you're diligent about honoring this time, it can be a game changer. Ask your partner for help with the morning feed, or use the first ten minutes of baby's nap time to do this (even if you have a laundry list of shit to get done).

- Listen to a podcast unrelated to parenting. This is something you can do when you're feeding or doing chores around the house. It's the little things that count!
- Get out and walk! This sounds like a no-brainer, but I was really good at finding excuses to sit inside and wallow in misery. Fresh air is always a good idea for you and for baby.
- Put on makeup. If you managed to shower, that is cause for celebration, but putting on makeup is a next-level achievement. Feeling good about how you look on the outside can help you feel more confident on the inside.
- Create an in-home spa. Tie a eucalyptus branch to your shower head, or drop some lavender oil in a bathtub. Pick up a new face mask or a yummy-smelling body scrub. I became a bath salts junkie (not literally) when I had my son, and taking baths helped my mind as much as it helped my muscles.

6

BIRDS OF A FEATHER PEE THEIR PANTS TOGETHER: FINDING YOUR MOM TRIBE

"Honey, you just gotta get through it."

It was sage advice—if, perhaps, a tad daunting—from my Great Aunt Alice to my mom on the night I was born, February 9, 1982. Despite my mother's sheer exhaustion from the twenty-hour labor when she pushed a small, feisty human (me) out of her body, something about the message resonated with her. For the next thirty-two years, my mother tucked away that bit of wisdom, and on the day of my own daughter's birth she decided to share it with me.

To the untrained eye, this had the makings of a tender moment between a mother and daughter, the passing of the maternal gauntlet, courtesy of my late Great Aunt Alice, who was an affable but gruff woman with the sort of graveled voice one develops after decades of smoking cheap cigarettes and a legacy that included petty theft (she was notorious for stealing restaurant cutlery and pocketing left-over bread rolls; in one unsubstantiated, albeit impressive, account, she successfully lifted an entire spiral ham from an Easter brunch buffet).

None of this should immediately disqualify her ability to provide sound parenting advice, but my mother failed to remember that years earlier she had shared another story about this particular aunt.

One afternoon in 1956, Great Aunt Alice dropped off her infant son at her sister's, my grandmother's, house so she could have a small break. My grandmother agreed to watch the baby, and he stayed with her . . . for the next two and a half months.

This is no exaggeration. Alice did not come back for him for ten weeks. When I reminded my mother of this and noted that the first few months with a newborn would be much easier if someone took your infant for that period, she bristled.

"Well, Leslie, she lived across the alley and would visit in the morning."

If this was intended to lessen the blow, it didn't. In fact, my great aunt's proximity to her abandoned newborn only seemed to make it that much worse that she had pawned him off on her sister.

At the time, I wondered what about having a child was so difficult that my great aunt left her infant son under the care of my grandmother, who was even less maternal than my own mother. (For the record, I adored my grandma, but she was also the woman who taught me what the term "cocksucker" meant when I was seven years old. Go ahead and chew on that for a minute.) As I grew in motherhood myself, I couldn't imagine leaving my newborn under the care of ANYONE else . . . even family.

For this book, I asked my mother to verify the facts of the story because they seemed a bit preposterous (even for my relatives). She confirmed that, yes, her mother took in my great aunt's infant, Cousin Russell, just a few weeks after he came home from the hospital. However, Mom made the amendment that her Aunt Marie (the oldest of the four sisters) also took turns caring for him, as Alice tried to "get her head on straight."

"Looking back now, I can see that Auntie Alice was really suffering," my mom recalled. "She was crying a lot and she wasn't sleeping, but we didn't call it postpartum depression or postpartum anxiety back then; my mother just said, 'she has the blues.' We didn't have doctors or professionals to help, so we just all pitched in."

To hear my mom tell it, Alice would come to the house every morning to feed the baby a bottle, and was fine for an hour or two, as long as someone was in the house with her. She didn't want to be alone.

"She would keep pulling the bottle out of his mouth every time he would make a little noise," my mom said, explaining how my great aunt feared her son would choke. "I remember sitting at the kitchen table with her and saying, 'It's okay, Auntie Alice, he does that all the time.' She laughed because, here I was, just eight years old, trying to make her feel comfortable with her own baby."

When the baby turned four months old, my grandmother told my Great Aunt Alice that it was time for her to take Russell home. She agreed, and back across the alley he went. But throughout the day, someone was always popping by—aunts, cousins, sisters, nieces—to make sure that both mama and baby were doing well.

It struck me as really remarkable how my grandmother recognized what was happening (likely before Alice even realized what was going on) and inherently knew that the most important thing was to help my aunt and her son survive those first few months. She wasn't an expert; she didn't have a stack of books or even a high school diploma. My grandmother just used the knowledge that was passed on to her when she brought home twin girls at the age of nineteen.

"People didn't take classes back then on how to take care of kids," my mom said. "We all just did what we thought was best and what our sisters, mothers, and aunts told us to do. At least, that's how it was in my family. We just did it together. My other aunt had a son years later, when I was nineteen years old, and I took a week off work to help her. It was just assumed that I would. We were family."

We've all heard the phrase "it takes a village," but never was it so profound to me than after my mom's retelling of this story. The modern mother is so overwhelmed with books, classes, and blogs that promise to enlighten her with all the information she'll need to manage new motherhood, but what new moms need most of all is support. We literally need warm bodies willing to hold our babies while we shower, nap, or eat. We need another mother who has walked the path before us to tell us what to do when our one-week-old has a crazy diaper rash or to say, "It's okay, use the gas drops," because everything we learned prior to baby has completely vanished from our minds. It's actually impressive how easily we can forget.

Raising a child was never supposed to be a solo journey for moms to experience in a vacuum but rather a team sport, where all members of your community pitch in. Yet, somehow today's mom is so isolated that she bears the burden of trying to "do it all." Our modern-day geography just doesn't afford us the same support new mothers had in previous generations. I don't know about you, but when I had my daughter I knew the names of only a few of my neighbors, and most of our encounters had revolved around cordial waves when our cars passed on the street.

My mother didn't live around the corner, and even though I was lucky enough to have her visit often during the first four weeks, that wasn't enough. New moms usually need around-the-clock care, just like our babies! And if a new mother doesn't have the initial support surrounding her in the early days and weeks, she's going to continue to struggle through the first months of motherhood. Ironically, we usually have women in our life willing and wanting to give us that support, but it's not always easy for us to ask for it. We've been trained to be a generation of "I got this" kind of girls.

THE IMPORTANCE OF THE MOM TRIBE

If you want to go to a tough hood, find a hood without a mom tribe. Motherhood is best served with warm hugs, tea cups, and empathic shoulders to lean on during those "what the fuck am I doing?" moments. Without this, we are left mothering and hustling in the wild, which is a pretty lonely way to do it. When you find a tribe, you are connected like a web. When one mama has a success, we all have a success. This new wave of mamas will lift you above the rising tide, and will meet you on the ship after with a tray of margaritas. These tribes, communities, circles, groups, and gatherings and the women who make them up remind us we are all on this journey together.

—KATYA LIBIN, cofounder of heymama, a global community for mothers in business

Certain cultures, recognizing this phenomenon, are trying to restore the balance. In places like South Korea and Hong Kong, postpartum recovery centers—most of them rather luxurious—are emerging, where new mothers can get the care they and their babies need during the early days of new mom life. France offers largely government-funded childcare to assist mothers going through this transition (although there is some debate about the ability for new moms to access it); France also offers new moms in-home checkups from nurses and doctors, which can be a huge lifesaver, as any new mom who has had to deal with "first doctor visit" stress can attest to. In China, they have a beautiful tradition of "sitting the month," which requires a new mom to do nothing for the first thirty days, while family and friends pitch in to handle housework, childcare, meals, and so forth. (In fact, many cultures have a similar tradition. In Latin America, it's called *la cuarentena,* a forty-day quarantine during which family rallies around to support the new mother; India and many Middle Eastern countries also subscribe to the forty-day lying-in philosophy.)

Yet for some reason, American women, despite their education and intelligence, ignore what history tells us and put on blinders to the rest of the world. Instead, many of us aim to tackle motherhood in the same way we approached our lives up until the point of conception: with drive, dedication, and impressive self-sufficiency.

Honestly, isn't that the stupidest thing you ever heard? I mean, I definitely thought that way before my daughter was born, but now that I have children, I can understand how ridiculous—and dangerous—that can become. Why are so many new mamas hell-bent on doing it by themselves? No one wins in that scenario. Trust me, I know this because I was one of the boneheaded mamas who was left to her own devices to explore new motherhood and try to do it on her own. Certainly, some moms have the foresight to plan a meal train and schedule their mom and mother-in-law trading off weeks for constant support, but I feel like that's the exception, not the rule (which is why I offer that exact advice in Chapter 3!).

Looking back, Great Aunt Alice wasn't a terrible mother, not even a little bit. Sure, the restaurant salt and pepper shakers somehow always ended up in her handbag, but that doesn't mean she didn't love her son fiercely; she was just struggling in this incredible life event. And when he passed away suddenly from a heart attack in his forties, she was beside herself with grief but pressed forward to fight—with every penny she had—to care for her young grandson, who had just lost his father. She had her quirks and faced her struggles, but she was a fucking awesome mom.

* * *

Beyond the inherent need for the experienced mamas in our familial community to rally around us to care for us during those early days, we also desperately need a community of mamas who are going through this new motherhood experience alongside us. Plenty of my friends had already ventured down the mom life road before me; they had all already emerged from those hazy, clumsy early days and could no longer relate when I was in the midst of it. It's not that they didn't try, but it's much like birth itself: when you're on the other side of it, you just tend to forget.

I remember yelling at my dear friend Jenny, who was an incredible source of support when new motherhood threatened to push me over the edge, when she couldn't manage to remember how many ounces of milk her daughter consumed at each feed when she was six weeks old.

"How can you not remember? It's literally all I think about!"

(Naturally, today I have absolutely zero idea how many ounces of milk Tallulah consumed during each feed at six weeks, but at the time it was my obsession.) What I truly needed was a community of mamas who were in the trenches with me during this crazy time; I needed my own band of mothers-in-arms.

Around the time Tallulah was eight weeks old, a friend suggested I join a mommy and me class. Initially, I agreed, but when it came time to actually go, I thought of every excuse I could to bail. I was tired, hormonal, and felt like a shell of myself. I wasn't sure I was capable of meeting new people, because I wasn't entirely sure who I'd be introducing them to—I really didn't know who this "new Leslie" was, or if I even liked her.

It's that catch-22 most new moms experience: it's a time in life when you feel isolated and crave interaction with humans other than your newborn, but getting out of the house and putting effort into forging a new relationship is the absolute last thing you want to do.

Lucky for me, my friend practically pushed me out the door for that first class.

"I'll go," I said, "but I'm not going to be happy about it." I distinctly remember choosing the most militant, don't-approach-me ensemble that I could pull together: a black shirt, dark gray moto pants, and black, gold-spiked combat boots. I was going for the "I'm not a people person" look.

When I arrived at the class filled with bubbly Santa Monica moms, I immediately felt like the oddball out. Not only was I not from the Westside (which is the equivalent of being a social pariah in Los Angeles), I also didn't seem to be jumping for joy over my new little bundle like everyone else was.

How could these women ever relate to what I'm going through? I peered at these cheerful-looking mamas, tucked smoothly into their lululemons and standing next to a row of pristine UPPAbaby strollers.

The instructor suggested that we go around the room and introduce ourselves and our babies and share what had been the biggest joy and biggest challenge of new motherhood. Mercifully, I was next to last.

The first few women confirmed my every nightmare:

"She's been basically sleeping through the night since week three," said one.

"I was told I could never have children, so this little guy is our miracle," said another.

"I'm loving every second at home and really trying to cherish this stage," said the third.

Fuck, I thought, frantically searching the walls for a fire alarm I could pull.

The next woman to speak was one of those tall, beautiful model types who was impossibly thin for normal life, which made the fact that she was only a few weeks postpartum seem like a cruel joke. I was determined to hate her guts.

She went through her entire intro without cracking a smile or revealing any hint of joy, and finally said: "I don't understand why he won't sleep." She sounded completely exasperated. "Like, he just screams all the time. I want to throw my head into a wall."

Oh my god, I thought. She was my people.

✣ ✣ ✣ AN ODE TO THE MAMA TRIBE

Understanding that the fog of newborn life is different for us all, I decided to ask a friend who I met during that baby group class to share her memories about those early days and why she decided to find her mama tribe. This is what Casey Leavitt, former model turned stay-at-home mom of two, said:

> For me, mommy and me class offered me such a sense of community. When I moved to Los Angeles, I didn't know anyone. The only mom friends I had were the wives and girlfriends of my husband's friends and most of their children were older, so joining a group was necessary. Being a first-time mom, I had no one to talk to; it was so isolating. You have nothing to compare it to, so you are just constantly questioning everything you're doing. Was it all in my head? Was I just being dramatic? I was alone all day and dealing with a high-needs baby. So, I *lived* for our baby group. It was the only time I was able to get out of the house and be with other people! Immediately, I fell in love with the group and the entire process. I remember reading the email where you told us you threw a shoe at your husband and I thought, "She's gonna be a good friend of mine." I liked it so much, I even joined a second mom group! And even all the annoying people with angel babies become part of your experience. They're all my people now.

✣ ✣ ✣

I sat through a few more candy-coated, overly saccharine introductions—I'm convinced these were total bullshit because it just isn't normal—before a brunette woman wearing a red bandana and overalls (about twelve months before overalls made a fashion-forward comeback) introduced herself. She stumbled through a quirky, charming intro, but it appeared her nerves were fraying in front of us. She explained that her son was born seven weeks premature, he spent some time in the NICU, and the anxiety of the trauma had taken its toll on her. On the floor next to her, a little man slept soundly in his car seat.

"He sleeps all the time," she gasped. "But I can't sleep. I'm waking up ten times a night to hover over him to see if he's breathing."

It was an eye-opening moment. I felt such compassion for her even though she had this seemingly easy baby. It was the very first time I realized that the difficulties women face in new motherhood aren't always because of the baby; sometimes it's just their own shit being amplified. It should have been obvious to me, but it wasn't. This trendsetting hippie couldn't enjoy how good she had it because of her own crazy little head. There are two types of friends I always look for: curmudgeons and crazies. And so far, these two ladies were speaking my language.

"If I can shower before noon, I'm popping the champagne," said another woman, blonde and sweet looking. All her physical traits told me she'd fall into the "motherhood is the hardest, most rewarding experience of my life" category of moms, but she surprised me. "Like, that's a major cause for celebration, because I can't seem to get anything else done in my life."

She didn't quite have the catastrophizing personality I prefer in new friends, but I decided to make an exception for anyone who could find a way to bring a drinking reference into a conversation about new motherhood.

I decided, then and there, that I had found my tribe. And four years later, they're still three of my favorite friends. (To hear them tell it, they were all a little terrified of me, the aggressive-looking biker chick in the corner with the stank face who kept referring to her newborn daughter as "homegirl.")

Over the next twelve months, we were each other's sounding board, resource center, and shoulder to cry on. We got together as often as we could, texted constantly, and saw each other at least once a week during class. Whether it was a sleepless night, a first cold, preschool mania, dropping a nap, or transitioning to solids, we were in lockstep with one another. Don't get me wrong, we each had different approaches and priorities, but we were all completely supportive of each other's journeys. That was the key.

YOU WON'T ACTUALLY GET A DIVORCE (PROBABLY)

Clutching my husband's iPhone, I walked toward our master bedroom window and, with impressive force, pushed the screen out of the frame.

"Leslie . . . don't," he warned.

It was too late. I was already committed. I looked him dead in the eyes and tossed his phone out the window and down onto our very brick, very hard patio approximately twenty feet below.

At the very least, I had the awareness to recognize that I was a walking, talking one-woman billboard for the "crazy bitch" stereotype, but it wasn't my fault. I had a seven-week-old baby, and my husband had the audacity, the absolute carelessness, to get sick. To become contagious, even, with the flu. Didn't he get his flu shot like I asked him to? He told me he did, but I wondered. Either way, his ailing condition prohibited him from continuing our nightly routine when he relieved me for a few hours so I could attempt to rebound my sanity. I needed that break. I depended on that break—and now it was being stripped from me.

He looked at me in astonishment but said nothing (not the response I was anticipating). He knew I expected him to react, so he decided not to—or maybe he just didn't have the energy to. Then again, it's not like he could be totally surprised; I had warned him.

Our daughter was a solid ninety minutes into her witching hour (note: the witching "hour" almost never lasts just sixty minutes), and I was doing my best to soothe her while trying to eat my dinner, wash out and sterilize a bottle, and get her spit-up-covered swaddle washed and into the dryer so it would be ready for bedtime. And my husband was just cozied up on the couch under a mound of blankets. I said, "If I have to watch you sit on the couch, acting as if you're dying of the flu, and reading ESPN on your phone, I'm going to fucking lose it." He put down the phone, but his hiatus was short-lived.

"If you're just going to sit there on your phone while I'm running my ass off, you might as well just go upstairs to bed," I spat.

He walked upstairs. I followed.

"Seriously? You're just going to leave me down there?" I yelled.

He had placed his phone, still aglow from recent use, on the dresser. That's when I got the brilliant idea to toss it out a second-story window. If I'm being honest, I wasn't upset with him for getting sick, I was simply irritated by his presence. The very *sight* of him was taking me to a dark place.

Our house was tiny, and I was bouncing around like a human pinball, back and forth from the nursery to the kitchen to the laundry, and all the while, he was just lounging on the couch and going about his life. When I suffered a bone-chilling bout of mastitis, I still managed most of the household duties as well as the baby. I guess what I'm saying is, I was jealous. I was crazy jealous because I did not have the luxury of being sick, and he did. The baby changed his life, certainly, but not nearly as much as it did mine. What's more, it was just assumed that my life would of course change *more* because I happened to have a uterus.

At the time, my husband's employer didn't offer an impressive paternity leave package; in fact, they barely allowed him the flexibility to work from home the first week after we had Tallulah. Unless you work for companies like Google or Netflix, mothers' partners usually aren't really given much time to be at home after the arrival of a baby. Only a handful of states have laws mandating paternity leave—five as of publication—but getting companies to comply can be tricky. To hear my husband tell it, "Business doesn't stop just because we had a baby."

Not to mention, most husbands and partners aren't keen to make demands and create waves at work when they now have a new family to support! It's a double-edged sword for our partners, and I really do try to appreciate that . . . even when I'm throwing shit out the window.

So, ten days after I had a baby extracted from my body, my husband left me to fend for myself. He spent his days talking to other adults, walking to Starbucks, and urinating in solitude; he was able to hold on to some pieces of his past life and create a bridge between his old and new worlds, and I began to resent it, like, a lot.

His world away from home sounded so liberated to me. Though logic reminded me that he had to continue working to support our family, I didn't always pay much attention to reason during those early days in newborn captivity. When he'd leave the house, I'd fantasize about his car ride. (Did he listen to talk radio or Pandora? Maybe he made a few phone calls? Or perhaps he sat silently, relishing the peace and quiet?)

He'd call to check in at midmorning, and I'd badger him about his lunch plan. (Was he going to pick up something at one of the cool markets in downtown LA? Would he sit on a bench outside the library? Or was he going out for a lunch meeting in the Arts District? What would he have? Would he get a beer too?) Then, around three o'clock, I'd start texting him about whatever daily disasters occurred in hopes of guilting him out of the office early so he could relieve me sooner than six or seven p.m. ("The baby shit on me twice, I still haven't been able to finish my coffee from this morning, the washing machine is broken, which means I have no clean burp cloths, and the dog ate the umbilical cord stump.")

I didn't recognize this at the time, but I felt abandoned by him. This adventure was something we planned to do together; having a baby was going to be this fifty-fifty deal. But it wasn't turning out that way. I was the one who carried her inside me. I was the one who gave birth. I was the one feeding her. And on top of that, I was the one handling just about everything else: making and attending doctor appointments; researching gadgets and formulas; ordering and reordering diapers and wipes; washing the clothes, the bottles, and the bed sheets I kept sweating through.

Even before Tallulah was born, I was the one doing most of the preparing—and it felt like the more things I handled, the less aware he became, even of the important shit. For example, in California, some hospitals suggest having your infant car seat professionally installed. They terrify parents-to-be with some obscene statistics, like 85 percent of all car seats are improperly installed, and then list all the injuries your child could experience if forced to ride in one of these mangled contraptions. You begin to feel like a negligent parent if you don't hire a professional (which is when they hand you the business card of an installation professional who will "save the life" of your unborn child for the nominal fee of $75).

Naturally, I had the car seats professionally installed in both our cars (when I finally surrendered my two-seater for the soccer mom mobile I was destined for), and because it was me, and not my husband, who attended these appointments, I was aware of how simple it was to snap the baby in and head home from the hospital for that very first drive. When it came time to leave the hospital, my husband stared at the car seat base—the silent passenger in his backseat for nearly three weeks—as if it were an alien. Instead of easily gliding the newborn carrier in until he heard that soft click, he tugged at the installation button until the professionally installed car seat popped out of place. To say I went berserk would be an incredible understatement.

All of my preparedness went out the window along with all my time spent. It wasn't just the fact that he messed up the car seat but also his inability to recognize how much effort I put into making our first drive home together smooth, seamless, and special. I did my part; I got the car seat safely installed and delivered the baby. All he had to do was click the carrier into the base. He desperately tried to salvage the moment and reinstall the base the best he could, but all I could think about was the hundred different ways she could die because of an improperly installed car seat. Eventually, I called my dad and asked him to drive my car—with a properly installed car seat base—to the hospital. It was a deflating moment for all of us and set the tone moving forward.

That day at the bedroom window, I realized this joint effort we embarked on together was turning into more of a one-woman show. I had reached my physical, emotional, and mental limit. It was his turn to pay the piper, and his iPhone became the sacrificial lamb.

As he turned to walk away—probably to go see if the phone was at all salvageable or smashed apart on our brick patio—I noticed a pair of his Nikes lying on the bedroom floor, roughly twenty-four inches away from the closet where they could have been put away. So close, yet so far. He clearly had no intention of putting away his shoes. Who did he think would? The same magical fairy who tiptoed into our house every night to quietly put his socks in the hamper and hang up the rogue leather belt slithering around the carpet?

As I covered the distance between the window and the shoes, I weighed my options. I could reach down, pick them up, and, with exaggerated effort, put them in his closet. But if tossing his phone out the window didn't get a reaction, I doubt putting away his shoes would either. I grabbed a shoe—and I'm not talking about no Nike Flyknit here; I'm talking about a thick, clunky-ass retro Air Jordan 2—and I threw it at him.

I was half aiming at his head and half aiming at the wall behind his head. If it hit him, I could feign ignorance: I meant to hit the wall, obviously, and his big-ass head had to get in the way. If it didn't, I always meant to hit the wall, so don't try to paint me out as this psycho!

Luckily for us all, my aim was total shit. It missed him by a solid foot and a half, and he zipped around on his heels and saw me standing there holding the other shoe.

"What the fuck, Leslie?" he shouted.

"Pack a bag and just go stay at a hotel!" I yelled back, only mildly committed to the idea.

"Because I have the flu? Get a hold of yourself!" he barked before walking out of the room.

IN DEFENSE OF YOUR PARTNER

Okay, I feel obligated to say that as much as husbands and partners can be the absolute worst, and even though you might lock yourself in the bathroom on occasion and give yourself a pep talk on how you could make it as a single mother, I must also tell you this: sometimes they can be pretty okay.

A few nights after the iPhone toss, my husband had made plans for us. (For the record, the phone miraculously and by the grace of God landed on an outdoor chair cushion and was completely unharmed.) He had gotten home early from work, asked my mom to come over, and told me to get dressed.

"Are you taking me somewhere to leave me for dead?" I asked. After my performance, it was a reasonable question. It also was very unlike him to make actual plans. I was the cruise director in the family, so the idea that he made any social decisions was alarming.

"No, we're going out," he said. "Get dressed."

"Where are we going?" I asked, anxious and excited, ready to shed the neon-pink SoulCycle sweatpants I'd been wearing for weeks, despite not having been to a spin class in three months.

He beamed with pride before announcing: "Ralph's!"

Ralph's is a chain of grocery stores in Southern California. A new two-story mega Ralph's—the kind with mini escalators for your shopping cart—had just opened about ten minutes from our house. Although this may sound like the worst place to take a woman on a date, for a new mother it was a dream come true.

We had only about an hour, door to door, so going to a movie or dinner was out of the question, and I was honestly ecstatic about the idea of casually and quietly perusing the aisles. I would make an extended stay at the cheese counter, asking to sample every soft cheese in the case. As soon as we had parked, I made my way to the fluorescent sliding doors like I was drifting toward the pearly gates.

But my husband grabbed my hand and pulled me in the other direction, toward the crosswalk.

"Come on, babe," he said. "We're going across the street for a quick drink first."

We grabbed two seats at the bar in the bustling pub, and I could feel my cheeks aching from the smile plastered on my face. I was out in the world . . . with other humans. No one in that bar knew I had a six-week-old baby at home. It felt like I had this huge secret, because to every other person there, I was just another girl at the bar with an enormous glass of pinot noir.

We made it back home an hour and ten minutes later. Tallulah was still sleeping in my mom's arms and I felt like a new woman. It's still the best date I've ever gone on.

✢ ✢ ✢

Yes, it was a pretty insane way for me to react, but I literally couldn't help myself. I needed him to be more interested in the whirlwind of chaos going on around him than in the start of the 2014 NBA season. I needed him to step the hell up and participate in this damn family. Why did he just assume it was all on me?

Not to get all "I'm a feminist, hear me roar," but how society views the modern family structure is pretty fucking archaic. I understand that, as a mother, there are certain things only I can do (carrying the baby, breastfeeding the baby, etc.), which often leads to a deeper connection between baby and mama. The deeper connection allows for a new mama to care for her baby and comfort her baby in a way no one else can. Beyond that, though, all the administrative shit that comes along with raising a human is pretty much up for grabs, but for some reason, I just adopted the role of "do-it-all" mama.

Modern patriarchy dictates that. No matter how evolved our relationships are, most couples just fall into these predefined roles of what it means to be Mom and what it means to be Dad . . . to which I call bullshit!

It may not feel totally obvious at first, but think about it. At restaurants, why do they have a baby changing table in the women's restroom and often not in the men's? If I'm out in public, with my kids and my husband, I'm never changing a diaper. It's literally the least he can do. On the cover of parenting books on sleep or discipline or first foods, why is it always a woman pictured with the baby? Even the font and lettering is swirly cursive and pink, which I don't think was intended to grab my husband's attention.

Shouldn't it be assumed that my husband wants to educate himself on raising our kids? Every diaper or baby soap commercial shows the mom giving the baby a bath. Where the hell is Dad? The strip club? Lots of working moms manage to bathe their children regularly. Can't it be assumed that a man can figure out how to do both as well?

After commiserating with other new mamas, I realized that many of us experience the same frustration over our seemingly endless duties as moms versus the role of our husbands. It doesn't take much for a mommy and me group to dissolve into a bitch sesh debating whose partner did the most bonehead thing.

It was during one such session that I came up with the "Parenting Pie Chart." The idea is fairly simple. When it comes to parenting, there are two equal halves: "Hands-On Care of Baby" and "Business of Caring for Baby."

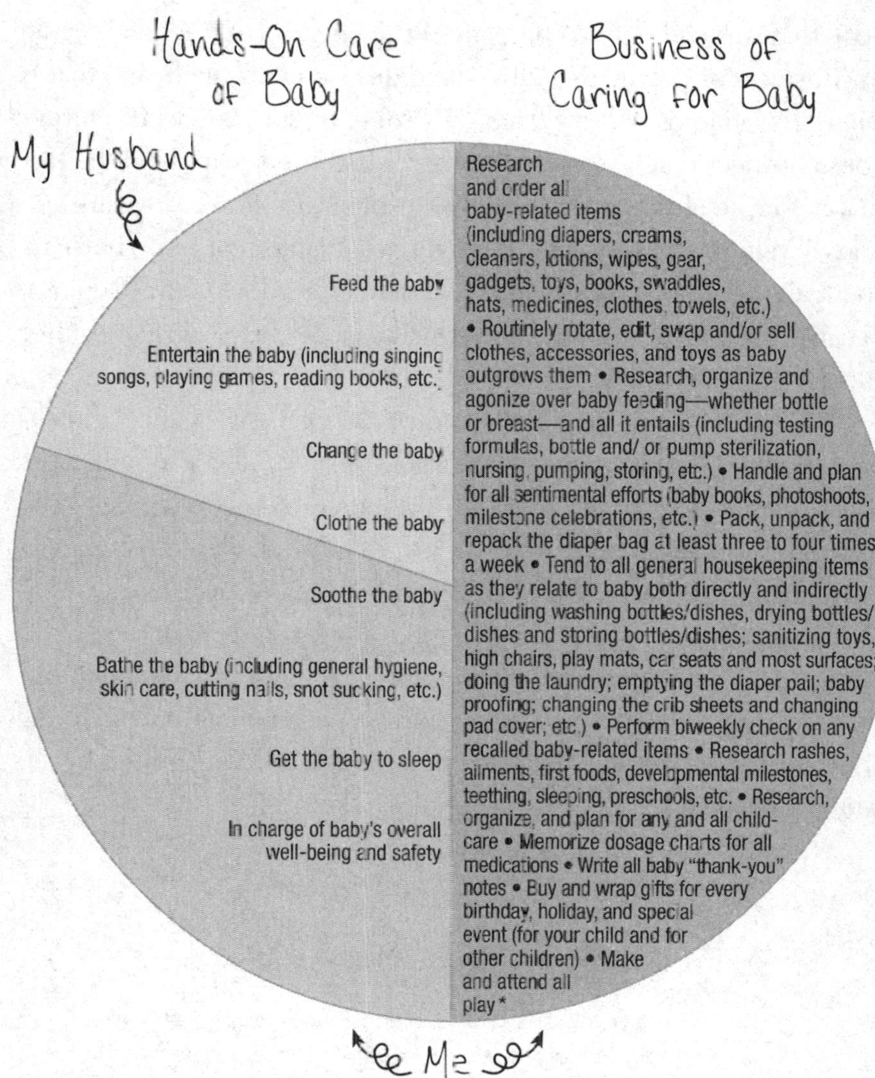

Despite what you might glean from these peeks into our marriage, my husband was really hands-on with Tallulah when she was a baby, but even if he took care of her 50 percent of the time (he did

*dates, baby classes, and doctor appointments • Plan all vacations, holidays, special events, and birthday parties • Pack for said outings and trips • Endlessly worry about the baby at all hours • Feel a suffocating and constant sense of guilt for not accomplishing everything on the list (in addition to general home care, self-care, relationship maintenance, and, perhaps, work).

Author's note: It is not lost on me that all of this text could not fit in the chart above.

not), that was still only 25 percent of the entire chart. When it came to "Business of Caring for Baby," he didn't do much at all, and that is where this animosity grew from. For some reason, our social culture doesn't expect much from guys either. I had friends applaud the fact that he stayed all three nights at the hospital with me . . . like, are you crazy!? Where else would he be? Even when our second was born, he spent all three nights with me. My parents stayed with our daughter, because it was over my dead body that he would leave me alone, after surgery, in the hospital with a newborn.

Realistically, my husband handled 20 percent of all Tallulah-related responsibilities, and I managed the rest—his was actually a pretty strong percentage, I found, compared to most partners. The remaining 80 percent rested on my exhausted, depleted, manic, postpartum shoulders. I can't tell you how often my husband likes to remind me how much more he does for our kids than most dads (although I'm not sure I totally buy this), which is great and all, but that means most dads aren't doing shit, because no matter which way you slice this parenting pie, 20 percent is still a failing grade. It's no wonder I was throwing phones out of windows!

A RESPONSE ARGUMENT FROM MY HUSBAND

Those first few months of fatherhood were a total trip. It was incredibly jarring to walk through the door of parenthood and have it close so swiftly—and so firmly—behind you. Mixed somewhere within the euphoria of looking at my bright, beaming daughter was the realization that *things done changed,* and life as I knew it was totally fucking over.

The new reality comes at you fast but also in waves—waves of bottles, diaper changes, runs to the store, hunching, shushing, applying lotions, and generally fumbling around in the dark.

My wife read *all* the books on new motherhood and infant care, so I figured she'd will herself into the zone and tow me along for the ride. Why study for the test when you're

> sitting shotgun to the girl with the winning Scantron? Of course, then when I saw my wife unraveling under the newness of parenthood, I thought that perhaps I should have been better prepared.
>
> Even though I felt like I embraced my new role as a dad, I didn't feel like I had any real confidence in what I was doing. I was there, I was willing, but I wasn't sure what lane my wife wanted me in. I was just trying to dodge flying objects long enough to keep my head on. I felt a bit lost in the moment, so to speak. It doesn't always come as natural to new dads, as it might for some new moms.
>
> In reality, nothing could have prepared us for being new parents other than going through it together, but if I could suggest one thing: communicate with each other. It sounds trite, but it's necessary. While having that open dialogue might not have always yielded a solution, perhaps we would have understood each other a bit more.
>
> Like, if you get the flu—the 102-degree fever full-on flu that people get preemptive shots to avoid and that has an entire season named after it—instead of dozing off on the couch and ultimately getting your phone thrown out a window, maybe you should take a beat to say, "I'm sick, and I know you're in it. I don't know how to help, because I know this is really hard for you. I love you, but I have the fucking flu."
>
> —YASHAAR AMIN, father of two, and the absolute love of my life

+ + +

Unfortunately, until our entire culture gets flipped on its damn ear, there's just not a ton we can do about it, because the learning curve for moms versus dads is just so wildly different. Think about it in terms of swimming lessons: different methods can be used to teach a parent to swim.

New fathers get a fairly gentle experience: the pool is heated to an agreeable 84 degrees, and they're given floaties and a kickboard for their twenty-minute session with a trained expert. New mothers, on the other hand, have it a bit tougher: they're taken out to the middle of the ocean . . . at night. It's dark, cold, choppy, and treacherous. They're tossed off the boat with a weighted belt. They're completely on their own and told to "sink or swim, bitch, sink or swim."

To survive new motherhood, women have to figure this shit out quickly. There's no other choice. We can't drag our feet on ordering new diapers because it will end up being our butts driving a poop-covered baby to the pharmacy at midnight. So we order the diapers, clean the bottles, do the laundry, cook the food, sterilize the pacifiers, and research diaper rash, all while feeding the baby, changing the baby, rocking the baby, and cleaning the baby. If any balls get dropped, we're the ones paying the price, so we quickly learn how to fucking juggle.

This imbalance only gets worse as time goes on because moms become so proficient at all things childcare. She can do in thirty seconds what might take her partner ten minutes, and our partners, bless their little hearts, get to take full advantage of our quickly sharpened skills. When disaster strikes, they have the support of a now seasoned professional. All of their hiccups, missteps, and oopsies come with an insurance policy: us.

Once when I asked my husband to change Tallulah's diaper, she came back to me still smelling like poop. I went to change her diaper again and realized he didn't throw out the old diaper! He put the new diaper on, but the old poop-filled one was folded up behind her bottom, along with the poopy wipe, all zipped back up into her onesie. Like, are you fucking kidding me? I would rather he forgot the diaper altogether. Thank goodness I was there, or my daughter would have spent her nap with a heat pack of her own crap pressed against her back.

STUPID SHIT YOUR PARTNER MIGHT DO (INSPIRED BY REAL EVENTS)

» Almost miss the delivery of your baby because he was getting his hair cut.

- Suggest that you drive yourself to the hospital to deliver, and ask that you scoop him up from the bar on the way there.
- Call an Uber to take you to the hospital so he can "have a roadie."
- Eat Doritos in your face during labor while you're forced to fast.
- Ask you, while still in the delivery room, to take a picture of him cutting the cord.
- Look below the sheet during delivery and tell you, "It's crazy down there!"
- Go home after your baby is born to shower and sleep, because labor was "really intense."
- Wear latex doctor's gloves to change your newborn's diaper.
- Forget to bring a car seat to the hospital, because he figured you would just hold the baby on the ride home.
- Eat his meals in the hospital cafeteria, because he needs some "alone time."
- Buy himself a push present.
- Rip the baby away from you while breastfeeding because he's afraid you're suffocating her.
- Go to a Phish festival for three days right after your baby is born, or to Myrtle Beach for a "boys weekend."
- Try to feed your two-week-old steak because she "looks hungry."
- Wear a Costco back brace for the first few months of your child's life because his back hurts from rocking her.
- Tell you that he needs to finish watching the NBA draft before he can drive you to your baby's first doctor appointment.
- Suggest establishing a firm routine for your three-week-old so he could resume his golfing schedule.
- Swaddle the baby's hands up to "hold the pacifier" in place. (This might actually be genius.)

- » Wash the baby's eye with soap during his first bath.
- » Put a newborn diaper on your toddler.
- » Get drunk with his friends and pass out in the crib.
- » Tell you the baby is crying and suggest you "do something about it."
- » Use the backyard hose on "jet" to rinse off your child after a diaper blowout.

Here's some truth salad: your relationship with your partner may suffer after the baby is born—and it might get pretty bad. As I write, I've been married to my husband for nine years and been together with him for seventeen (which is preposterous when I think about it. How am I old enough for that to be possible?), and the most challenging period of our marriage was the first year after our daughter was born. For a while, we were coexisting, but not intersecting.

He and I functioned on different planes; we just couldn't get through to each other because we were blind to the other's journey. He didn't understand why I couldn't appreciate how challenging it was for him to be at work all day and then come home to a chaotic house, an exhausted wife, and a cranky baby, while bearing up under the financial pressure of being the sole breadwinner until I took my next job.

I didn't understand why he thought I would fucking care about any of that. How could his workload and daily stresses possibly compare to the emotional and mental breakdowns I was having on the regular while acting as the sole caregiver to a human fucking being? How could his familiar routine compare to the feeling of being dropped in the wilderness with no idea how to escape?

He had every right to feel the way he did. Under normal circumstances, that's a heavy burden for a person to carry. But it's *nothing* when compared to new motherhood. And, as a woman, if you're already feeling underappreciated and unseen, this kind of shit can really make you come unglued. I didn't understand why it was all on my shoulders; I didn't understand how he couldn't see it. How could he be so oblivious?

Look, I appreciate that men have their own journey into fatherhood, and it can feel confusing for a lot of new dads. A lot of men don't feel connected to the baby or even their partner in the early days. They struggle to find their place in this new dynamic. It's an intense transition. In fact, someone should probably write a book on it because it deserves to be explored more, but it sure as hell ain't the point of this one. I'll help explain the dad journey as it relates to moms, but if a dad is gonna use his struggles as an excuse not to throw in a load of laundry . . . to the left, to the left.

GIVE THE DADDY A DUTY

Just the title of this is a bit annoying. Yes, your husband should have many duties, but in the early days it can be challenging to separate yourself long enough to give him the chance. A friend gave me some advice. She told me to make my husband do bath time every single night. She told me that I could *not* stay in the room to supervise. I had to trust in my heart that my husband loved my child as much as I did and that he wouldn't do anything life-threatening.

At first, I wanted to micromanage the situation (Was the water temp at exactly 99 degrees? Was he using the hypoallergenic, organic baby soap? Was he cleaning the appropriate parts? Did he have a warm washcloth over the baby's belly to prevent a chill? Did he know which lotion to use afterward?). Eventually, after a few weeks, my husband not only got comfortable with the bath but also became a lot more self-assured in his daddy duty role in general. After implementing this rule, on the rare occasion that I did help with bath time, my husband constantly corrected me.

"No, Leslie, she doesn't like that washcloth, she likes this one."

"This shampoo does *not* react well with her skin. Get this out of here."

And so on, and so on.

I wanted it to annoy me, but I was actually pretty happy that he had found such confidence with this small corner of our baby's world. It was one less thing for me to worry about, a chance for me to eat dinner with two hands, and an opportunity for them to bond. Not to mention, handing my husband responsibilities straightaway was a good way to set the tone for the following weeks and months. The faster he got comfortable with managing the baby, the more he could do. Unless, of course, he gets the flu.

8

THERE IS NO *I* IN MOTHERHOOD: SURRENDERING TO YOUR POSTPARTUM IDENTITY CRISIS

"God is fucking with me," I muttered under my breath.

After twenty-four hours of hot compresses, constant feedings, pumping, and writhing pain, my nipple blister finally decided to burst at the worst possible time. Every day, I could manage about forty-five minutes of freedom, and I chose this day to run to the store for more nursing bras, and while standing on line to check out, I suddenly felt a massive release of pressure.

Perfect, I thought. I looked down and saw an embarrassing large wet spot form across my left boob; of course, today was the day I chose a light gray T-shirt and forgot disposable breast pads. I approached the register, clutching two nursing bras, and smiled through clenched teeth at the A Pea in the Pod sales associate.

"Milk blister," I offered, trying to remain casual. She nodded sympathetically.

"I hope your day gets better," the associate said, handing me a paper bag.

"Me too," I said, clutching it to my chest before heading to the door.

Who was I kidding? How was my day going to get better? This outing was supposed to be the highlight: a full hour out of the house!

By the time I got to the car, I could feel my entire body deflate—along with my boob. I stared at my reflection in the driver's side window but didn't recognize the disheveled, greasy, overweight woman staring back at me.

Who had I become in this whole motherhood miracle? I mean, I knew I had brought new life into the world, but did that somehow mean I had to forfeit mine?

For more than a decade, I fought to build the life I wanted, but now I felt it slipping away.

My pre-baby life was largely ordinary, but, at times, totally unbelievable. Like many women my age, I spent much of my adolescence and college years watching *Friends* and *Sex and the City* and developed a fascination with New York City. After graduate school, I hoped to pursue a career in publishing, so I made the dramatic cross-country move to Manhattan to work as a reporter for *Us Weekly* magazine. My particular beat was nightlife and events; in other words, my job was to go out . . . a lot.

For a twenty-four-year-old, life didn't get much sweeter. Sure, I spent most days stepping over puddles of urine and eating drug-store frozen burritos for dinner, but I was too young to care. Over the next few years, my job took me all over the world and gave me entrée to some of the most glamorous events, like the Academy Awards and the Cannes Film Festival. By 2010, I was living in Los Angeles full-time and took a job as a senior writer for *The Hollywood Reporter,* a trade publication for the entertainment industry; the opportunity put me in front of moguls and superstars alike. The hours were long and the work was often insurmountable, but I felt empowered and productive. I was a #girlboss!

But becoming a mom levels the playing field for all of us.

In 2014, we welcomed Tallulah into the world and everything changed.

Motherhood is a sacrifice, an adage I must've heard a hundred times before becoming a parent. Surely, it would be a sacrifice of time, resources, and personal commitments; what I didn't realize is that it would also be a tremendous sacrifice of self. Everything I was prior to baby suddenly became less important (if any part of my former self happened to still exist at all). Once that epiphany hit, I could feel the walls closing in around me. For me, my pre-baby "identity" was defined by my strong relationships, my desire to travel, my need to be active, my work, and, most importantly, my alone time. I spent thirty-two years discovering and defining myself as a woman and, in becoming a mom, I felt forced to abandon that identity.

"I think something's wrong with me," I told my husband. I couldn't understand why I wasn't insanely happy. I felt lonely and isolated. Despite the countless hours in the day that chugged along at a slow trot, I never managed to find any time to do anything besides care for Tallulah. How could it be that the days felt never-ending but I could never manage to accomplish anything?

My life used to be my own, but now my entire existence centered around this tiny little human.

For many new moms, the identity loss is crippling. You spend your entire adolescence and adult life trying to figure out who the hell you are as a person, what you're good at, and where you fit in. It's only logical that a woman with a strong sense of personal identity is going to suffer when her new role as mother forces her to abandon many of the "things" she felt once defined her. Not to sound bleak, but women must grieve the loss of their former lives, of the independence they once knew.

And I think this is where we struggle, because saying that out loud is scary. We wonder whether these feelings of self-loss and confusion are somehow indicative of how much we care for our children.

If I say I'm having a hard time with motherhood, will people think I don't love my baby?

Girl, you know better than that. When I was in the weeds with my little Lu, I asked myself the same thing and I wish someone had told me to wake the fuck up. Like I said in the beginning, you can experience two conflicting feelings, and one does not beget the other. But I also know that's easier said than done.

We talked about this a bit in Chapter 2, but since many women today struggle to have children, new mothers don't always feel "allowed" to have a hard time. Therefore, they don't vocalize how challenging it can be because they're terrified of being judged or made to feel ashamed. And you know what? That's total crap.

Listen to me now: someone else's experience doesn't dictate yours. Just because other women struggle with their journey, you're still allowed to share your own motherhood experience without being made to feel bad. Just because you were so very blessed to carry a beautiful, healthy baby to term doesn't make it any less challenging when your child is up all night long sobbing because he's cutting his first tooth and is only quiet when you're rocking him. And, chances are, you have a big meeting or deadline or appointment the next day . . . because that's just how shit works.

If your home gets broken into or your car gets rear-ended, are you not allowed to be upset because you are lucky enough to have a home and a car in the first place? Of course not.

By the way, the same thing could be said for women struggling with fertility. When I shared my pain to conceive my second baby with a woman who wasn't yet a mother, she told me, "Be happy you at least have your daughter." Girls, let's just stop competing over everything. Even our sorrow has become a platform for comparison. Ugh!

Change is always hard, and you're going through the biggest change in your life—physically, emotionally, and even logistically! You are becoming a new version of yourself, you're becoming a mom, and that's not easy. It takes time to find your groove, and you will get there. You will fall in love with the new you, but it takes time.

Don't get me wrong. I understood that having a baby meant the most exciting parts of my life were behind me—I mean, not initially, but I figured it out pretty quickly. What I didn't expect was how challenging my day-to-day life would become. Even the small parts of my ritual would become burdensome; I couldn't manage to finish a cup of coffee before it went cold, I couldn't get out of my pajamas before noon, and I could rarely finish a single chore before something else diverted my attention. Even with Tallulah securely in her bassinet, I would find myself rocking as I slapped together a sandwich, the sense memory of having her in my arms. The juggle was oh so real. My new world consisted of round-the-clock feedings, chronic gas, sweatpants, baby bottles, diaper cream, burp cloths, topknots, empty food wrappers, and involuntary home confinement.

I missed being needed in any capacity beyond "milk machine," "professional shusher," or "butt wiper." I longed for grown-up conversation that had nothing to do with how many ounces a fill-in-the-blank-week baby should be consuming and when to switch to solids.

I'd hear about my friends having lunch dates or movie nights that I was no longer invited to. My husband would have obligatory work dinners, while I ate a tuna fish sandwich over my nursing daughter's head, and when a glop fell out of the sandwich and into her mouth, I spent the whole night googling "tuna poisoning in newborns."

We'll talk about the struggle to accept your new "mom bod" in Chapter 12, but that plays a pretty big role in this identity crisis too.

Each of us came to the class with different questions and concerns, but we were all looking for the same thing: community. We were no longer alone.

Depending on where you live and the resources available to new mothers, it might not be easy to find your own new mama tribe, but I assure you it's worth every effort. If you're looking for resources, it's as simple as googling "mommy and me classes" near you. If using the internet as your beacon of light feels a little shady, ask your doctor or pediatrician for a list of resources in the area. Most hospitals and midwiferies offer some sort of postpartum support for new moms. You may even check out your library's story time (they tend to be pretty popular) or join a local infant gym or music class. I promise you, the resources are there if you're willing to look.

The important thing is to find other mamas with children close in age to your child's. Take it from me, your best friend with the eighteen-month-old won't be able to commiserate with you about building up milk supply or your fourth straight sleepless night—they're too caught up with toddler tantrums and trying to keep their child from running into walls. I even encourage mamas to use social media, discerningly, to find Facebook groups and even Instagram accounts that speak openly and honestly about the motherhood experience (ahem!). Making new friends isn't always the easiest thing to do, but it can be the "hardest, most rewarding experience" of your life.

New moms are on the front lines—dodging full-loaded diaper grenades and wielding nipple shields—without any real form of defense or, more importantly, community. Today's new mother is set up for failure without the structure of a village around her to guide her through this incredible transition. I realize now that my crazy-ass Great Aunt Alice was right. I just needed to get through it. And for me, that meant turning to the people around me for three minutes, three days, three months, or three years.

Before Tallulah, working out was a priority. Look, I'm not one of those "I love working out" girls; like most people, I dread every second of it. That being said, as a thirty-one-year-old woman without kids, I was confident in my skin for the first time in my life, and being active was a huge part of that.

In the early days after Tallulah was born, exercising simply wasn't possible and the easiest meal was always takeout or frozen pizza. I didn't even have time to make my bed; how the hell could I manage to prepare a week's worth of healthy, breastfeeding-friendly, detoxifying meals? I'm not Gwyneth Paltrow!

I knew the steps I needed to take to start to reclaim my former appearance, but I didn't have the time to take them. (For the record, if you ever really want to feel like a fucking shell of a human, try putting on your "regular" jeans three weeks postpartum. It'll really mess you up.)

It's hard being completely at the service of another human, who for the first few months doesn't really give much back. Sure, they're cute and cuddly and a miracle—blah, blah, blah—but newborns don't smile when you walk into a room or reach out to give you a hug. Typically, they spend most of their time eating, sleeping, pooping, and crying. My mom actually said it best: "For the first three months, your only job on this planet is to keep them alive." I just didn't realize there wouldn't be any coffee breaks.

I've often compared motherhood to a less brutalized, less dark version of *A Handmaid's Tale*. During her infancy, I was "OfTallulah." She was my keeper and my life's purpose was to be at her beck and call, to fulfill her needs, sacrificing all of mine. I was a vessel to ensure her happy and healthy life. If you've seen the show or read the book, you'll know that comparing your newborn to a tyrannical world order where women are made to be sex slaves may seem a bit harsh . . . but if you have kids, you'll also know it's some real truth salad.

Motherhood can be really taxing on a woman, and because we're ashamed when we don't feel a certain way about our new motherhood experience we suffer in silence. I watched, with hopelessness, the beautiful, Instagram-worthy motherhood experience of everyone around me and how casually they seemed to marry together their pre- and postbaby lives. My pregnancy was textbook and my daughter was the picture of health, so I didn't feel like I had the right to feel the way I did. I continued to hide behind a forced smile, but inside I felt so completely alone.

The moral of the story isn't to keep you from having children altogether or to force you into the complete resignation of your former self but rather to help you to understand that what you're feeling is *common,* that you are not the only woman to feel this way, and that it does work itself out. Periods of transition are just that . . . periods. It's not forever, and you will come through it. Though it may not make things easier in the moment, it can make it feel a lot less lonely.

As soon as I opened up to other moms about my identity loss in the weeks and months postpartum, I realized that I wasn't the only one suffering the *exact same feelings*—and there really is no substitute for the empathy and understanding of other women who have been there.

"It's hard for everyone," my friend Erin told me after I finally opened up to her. "We all struggle; it just doesn't always look the same for you as it does for someone else."

Instantly, I was no longer the worst mom on the planet. In fact, I was just a new mom who was trying really hard and doing my best but still fumbling on occasion like everyone else. I had great days and hard days, and having bad days didn't make me a bad mom. I was just figuring it all out.

In many ways, we're not unlike our new babies. We're being born into new roles and a new way of life. And just like our children, we're learning about the world around us, and it's frustrating when we can't quite make all the puzzle pieces fit together. It takes some time to adjust. We need to learn to accept the painful realities of the moments that will be missed, the clothes that will no longer fit, and the world that no longer rotates on its axis for us alone. We have to come to grips with letting go of the life we had before.

But, in letting go of one thing, we're opening ourselves up for something new. Once you've navigated the murky waters of infant land, you're gonna realize that this new life with this new person is pretty fucking incredible. Your new little boy or girl gets to set off into this world and discover who he or she is, just as you once did, but now, you get the awesome power of exploring it together and guiding your child along the way.

And you want me to let you in on a really huge secret? You might start to like yourself more as a mom than you ever did before. Being responsible for another human life has taught me a lot, especially patience. I'm more patient today than I ever thought possible. I also have a deeper compassion and understanding for others, and I like that about myself. As corny as it sounds, my daughter made me a better person. In December 2017, there was a devastating wildfire north of Los Angeles. Families lost everything just weeks before Christmas. I thought of all those moms and decided to help. Tallulah and I went to Target and picked out everything we could to refurnish a new bedroom for a little girl her age, right down to the mattress. I want to believe I would have done the same thing before having kids, but I don't think that's true. I had empathy because, as a mother, I love my child more than I do myself, and I couldn't imagine the repercussions of such devastation. Becoming a mom has taught me how to have a care for others more than a care for myself, and that's a pretty huge gift.

It's going to get easier, this whole "becoming a mom" thing. I had a pretty great life before I started my family, and I recognize that. These days, I don't often get to put on makeup and high heels, but you know what? I don't really give a shit anymore. Sure, there will be stuff about your old life that you'll miss, but the incredible moments you'll have in this new chapter outweigh them by a ton. When you hear your baby girl laugh for the first time or watch your baby boy start to crawl, it's like magic. I can't properly put into words what it feels like to witness them become their own little people who squeal with excitement when you walk through the front door, who make terrible jokes like, "Mom, you're a car wash head," who hide behind the couch during a particularly intense episode of *Paw Patrol,* who ask insane questions like, "Why are houses made of wood?," who swell with pride the first time they put together a puzzle on their own, and who squeeze their eyes shut with tremendous dedication to make a wish before blowing out the candles on their birthday cake. And I will tell you that when your son scrapes his knee for the first time, or your daughter gets a bad stomach bug, there is literally nowhere on this planet that you would rather be than by their side. Not even the Cannes Film Festival or the Academy Awards.

SHIT YOU SHOULD KNOW: HOW TO GO BACK TO WORK

Being self-employed and working from home has its fair share of challenges—especially when your occupation requires a relatively quiet atmosphere and your toddler is resisting potty training with the fire of a thousand suns. That being said, it also allows me a reasonable amount of flexibility. With you working mamas in mind, I reached out to my friend Sydney Gilbert, who has overseen marketing at several different high-profile lifestyle brands, including TOMS and Beyond Yoga, while her family grew.

Sydney has insight in managing the transition back to work mode, saying:

> I spent most of my maternity leave panicking about going back to work. It was all-consuming and I couldn't shake it—even though I was "being paid to be on vacation" with my newborn (as one of my child-free female

> coworkers so compassionately put it). I kept wondering: *Do I have to return? What will my job look like? Should I even return to work at all? Who will care for my kid? Am I working just to pay someone to watch him? Is day care a petri dish of germs? But I can only afford a petri dish. What are my other options? Do I quit? How could I leave my child with a virtual stranger? Would he grow up thinking she was his mom? Would he love her more than me?*
>
> Being a working mom means you're going to fall victim to mom guilt. We question ourselves and our decisions; we begin to foster resentment and shame. It's a mourning process, and every working mom must go through it. I knew I'd eventually find some sort of balance. Some days I was a better worker than others, and some days I was a better mom . . . but I learned to go easy on myself. It's not easy having two jobs. Above all else, remember this: *You will always be the mom. No one can replace you.*

Since Sydney had her two children while working at two very different companies, she has a wider breadth of experience than most, and I just knew she would have the best advice and suggestions to help all you mamas looking to navigate these back-to-work waters.

1. Find childcare that works for *you*.

   Every option comes with a host of stigmas, so the best thing you can do is choose what is right for your family. Whether it's a nanny, a nanny share, or day care, Sydney says, "Don't be so hard on yourself when it comes to making this choice; each has its perks and each has its pitfalls."
2. Talk to other working moms. They will be your best resources.
3. Establish a morning routine.

   "Having a plan saves you from major headaches later," she says. The key is communicating with your partner and your caregiver, and even setting a plan for yourself so everyone knows what is expected.

4. Write out a schedule and rules.

   Worrying about your child while you're gone is inevitable, but it makes the transition a lot easier when everyone knows the game plan. Make sure the caregiver knows your child's routine and what you expect from him or her (e.g., no media, no napping in stroller, whatever).

5. Expect to miss the "firsts."

   "It's a shitty feeling, but it happens," Sydney says. "You should prepare yourself for it early; it lessens the blow."

6. Prepare to pump.

   Because what mom doesn't want an extra bag to carry? Remember to pack your pump, clean pump parts, pump wipes, storage bags, a cooler, and ice packs. Also, if you can, invest in a hands-free bra and a car adapter for your pump. Make the most of rush hour!

7. Get baby used to the bottle.

   "A few weeks before, have someone other than you feed the baby at least once a day with the bottle," Sydney suggests. "You don't want the stress that comes with the news that your baby isn't taking one."

8. Communicate with colleagues and know what you are entitled to.

   Transitioning back is a major challenge, so talk to your boss (and HR if you have one) about what this looks like. Don't be afraid to ask for a little leniency the first few weeks—you just had a baby! And the worst thing they could say is no (literally, the worst). Also, employers are legally required to allow you time to pump as well as a private space to pump. Tell them your pumping schedule, and be firm.

9. If you're done pumping, be done.

   On the same note, if you've tried and it's just too much, give yourself the grace to stop (without all the guilt).

10. Be a mom leader at your job.

    "Chances are you are not going to be the only person at your company to have a baby, so help the organization realize how they can support moms," Sydney suggests. "Normalize that this is your new normal, and should be for other moms. Know your rights as a new mom. Talk to your boss and your HR department to let them know what you expect of the organization. Don't be afraid to speak up!"

✣ ✣ ✣

It took some time getting used to, and it's not all sunny days, but life with my children is better than anything I had before. You might not feel the same right now, but you will. I promise. And it's going to be fucking awesome.

9

HOW YOU FEED YOUR BABY IS NOT UP FOR PUBLIC DEBATE. PERIOD.

My husband handed me the orange prescription pill bottle of antibiotics that had already halved my milk supply once before. It turns out that mastitis—a common breastfeeding complication that I had never heard of before having my daughter—is no fucking joke, and I was well into my second battle with it.

I knew I needed to take the medication, but I also knew that taking it could further reduce my already crippled milk supply. The infection developed rapidly. It was two weeks before Christmas, and I snuck out to the mall to do a bit of shopping. About twenty minutes into the errand, I could sense something was wrong. By the time I got home, I was already sporting a pretty impressive temperature. My husband immediately called my OB, who had a prescription sent to the pharmacy and directed him to get it as soon as possible.

"Have some water," he said, handing me a glass and encouraging me to take the pills.

As I lay in bed shivering and convulsing from the now 103-degree fever, *It's a Wonderful Life* taunted me from the television like an incredibly unfunny punch line. I briefly considered risking my own health and not taking the pills. I sobbed each time I tried, in vain, to feed my hungry, tiny baby. She was so pure and so small, how could I possibly fill her body with formula? How could I let her ingest something manufactured in some factory instead of from my own body?

I wasn't ready to stop breastfeeding. I kept hearing the vicious echoes of other women, and all the horrible things that could potentially happen to my daughter as a result of what I considered my maternal incompetence. If some horrible illness were to befall her at the age of ninety, it would undoubtedly be because of my inability to breastfeed her for longer now. What if she develops allergies? What if her immunity suffered?

(I want pause for a second to say that formula is not toxic, and I'm a logical woman who should have recognized this at the time. I'll talk much more about this shortly, but I was allowing myself to fall down an unnecessary rabbit hole that only made things worse.)

Breastfeeding had by no means come easy to me. In fact, as I mentioned earlier, I wasn't entirely sure I wanted to breastfeed Tallulah. And saying that openly isn't an easy thing to do, especially in a culture that makes it acceptable for friends, family, and even strangers to shame women who aren't breastfeeding:

"Ooh, I hope that's breast milk in that bottle . . ."

"I'd never formula feed my baby."

"Why didn't you keep trying?"

"It's our job as women and mothers to breastfeed."

"Breast is best!"

It wasn't that I didn't want to do what was considered best healthwise for my child, but breastfeeding is serious business, and it requires serious work. Mostly, my insecurities drove my hesitation. I had been subjected to enough horror stories—and sob stories—that I was terrified of the very idea. I watched, helplessly, as my best friend writhed in pain as she tried to nurse her newborn son on one breast while holding a blood-soaked paper towel to the other. I comforted another friend as she crumbled in excruciating defeat and disappointment after realizing her body wasn't producing enough breast milk to feed her child. I got recommendations for countless products that promised to aid in all the potential breastfeeding woes (of which there are many), and I heard story after story about how time-consuming, painful, and often discouraging the whole process could be. I was also anxious that it would forever ruin my boobs (yes, that's totally vain, but it was a legitimate concern). When I mentioned to my husband that breastfeeding may not be for me, I could tell it bothered him.

He didn't say anything at first, treading lightly, as most expectant fathers tend to do, and then chose his moment carefully. He told me that breastfeeding was really, really important to him and that although he would never pressure me into any decision when it came to my body, he really wanted me to reconsider it.

I'm not going to lie; this really annoyed me. My husband is a remarkable father, but when it came to "planning" for baby, he never bothered to open a book. All of the looming childcare decisions somehow fell on my shoulders—on top of actually CREATING HUMAN LIFE IN MY BODY—yet he somehow had an opinion on whether I should attach a human head to my body for countless hours.

After my initial annoyance subsided, I considered his request. Although he wasn't necessarily going over nursery checklists or researching nontoxic, zero-VOC paint options, he was very grateful and appreciative of the fact that I had taken the reins, and he had total faith in me to make these big decisions. He trusted me, and I had to give him credit for that. However, like me, he had been bombarded with information about the benefits of breastfeeding—and how formula is largely considered rat poison—and was nervous that our little girl might develop some completely preventable disease because we made the selfish, lazy choice to formula feed. (I hope you're sensing my sarcasm here.)

SHIT YOU SHOULD KNOW: BREASTFEEDING STATISTICS*

Babies ever breastfed: 82.5 percent

Still breastfed at 6 months: 55.3 percent

Still breastfed at 12 months: 33.7 percent

Breastfed exclusively through 3 months: 46.6 percent

Breastfed exclusively through 6 months: 24.9 percent

*Statistics from the Centers for Disease Control and Prevention: https://www.cdc.gov/breastfeeding/data/facts.html

Basically, he was a victim of the same shame game that I was, and actually had our child's best interests at heart (whether or not his concern was valid is another story).

Well, shit. If he felt that strongly about it, then I would absolutely reconsider. Perhaps his voice was what I needed to hear to force myself to move past my hesitations and fears. It had obviously been weighing on him, and he took the time to address it with me in a thoughtful way.

Not all people have horrible breastfeeding experiences, I told myself. Some people actually love it! Maybe I would be one of those women. I knew that the health benefits of breast milk were unparalleled, and that it had the potential to be an incredible bonding experience. Just because I didn't like the way people kept pressuring me to breastfeed shouldn't mean that I abandon the idea out of spite.

I told my husband that I wanted to do what was best for my baby, and that maybe he was right. Perhaps breastfeeding would be the best choice for us. I shouldn't just assume it wouldn't work before even giving it a try. That said, if complications came up or if it became too stressful, I asked if he would respect my decision to stop. He emphatically agreed.

Because of all of my breastfeeding-related anxieties, I decided to take a lactation seminar with a woman who was considered the breastfeeding guru of Los Angeles. The workshop was held in the back room of a one-stop baby shop in a Hollywood strip mall, an unimpressive venue, to say the least. I plopped down in a plastic folding chair along with twenty other expectant women, glossy white folder in hand that promised to be my breastfeeding bible. A professional, stern-looking woman took her place in front of us. There appeared to be nothing warm or fuzzy about the woman who was going to teach us about the intimate miracle of sustaining human life with our boobs. How tall she seemed, perched on that stool and peering down at us, like a breastfeeding Gandalf.

Actually, she reminded me more of a stuffy elementary school principal who got some sort of cheap thrill from her position. She asked us to introduce ourselves one by one and actually interrupted one woman (let's call her Marcia) to tell a "funny story" about how the instructor's own mother always thought the name Marcia should belong only to "hookers."

Talk about a warm welcome.

For the next two hours, she offered us a crash course in breastfeeding: how to prepare, what gear to procure, which positions worked best, problem-solving tactics, and so forth. She even suggested that each of us whip out our nipples so she could have a gander and recommend the ideal size breast pump suction cup.

I would have been happy if the class ended right there. I had gotten what I came for and was ready to go home. But, no. On top of the practicalities of breastfeeding—which is why a bunch of moms-to-be drove into Hollywood at rush hour—this arrogant woman gifted us with a thirty-minute homily of opinion and judgment. She shared with this group of hormonal, impressionable women, who had come seeking advice and counsel, that if we did not breastfeed, we were threatening our child's emotional, mental, and physical health. Any ailment a baby could possibly contract would somehow be the result of our decision not to breastfeed. I'm not exaggerating: she was charged, aggressive, and seemingly intent on scaring the hell out of us. If breastfeeding was too challenging and we chose to give up, we were quitters and lazy mothers. Not only was breastfeeding best; breastfeeding was the only way anyone should feed their child.

I couldn't believe my ears. Was this bitch serious? I looked around the room at the twenty-plus women (and some men) who had come here for support and guidance. They stared at the instructor with terror in their eyes. Statistics show that at least half of the women in that room would supplement their child's diet with formula within the first three months of life, and a few would not be able to breastfeed at all. This instructor knew those statistics, so what the fuck was she doing?

How would the women who needed to supplement receive that news now that they had the judgmental criticism of this breastfeeding drill sergeant rattling around in their heads? This instructor was terrorizing these mamas-to-be into breastfeeding submission. An already stressful situation can go from challenging to fucking apocalyptic when so-called experts use their position of power to browbeat women. (When it comes to motherhood, there is an "expert" for every school of thought. Whatever methods you believe to be best, there are professionals out there to support your beliefs, and just as many ready to tell you how very wrong you are.)

EXPERT ADVICE YOU DEFINITELY SHOULD *NOT* LISTEN TO

"There is no reason for believing that a woman who smokes moderately, let us say ten cigarettes or less a day, need change her custom at this time. If you have been used to smoking considerably more than this for several years, by no means try to give them up in pregnancy."

—Dr. Nicholson J. Eastman
in *Expectant Motherhood*, 1940

"Many babies today start enjoying Gerber's Baby Cereals as early as five or six weeks!"

—Mrs. Dan Gerber
in *Parents' Magazine: Baby Care Manual*, 1952

"Some mothers and experienced nurses insist that a fretful or tense baby is much happier if he sleeps in a small space . . . even a cardboard carton filled with a folded pad and lined with a blanket."

—Dr. Benjamin Spock
in *Baby and Childcare*, 1957

"Never forget to give the baby cooled boiled water regularly. This is frequently overlooked and time and again restless crying babies have been quieted by simply slackening their thirst . . . Never indefinitely nurse a baby. When teeth appear, it is approaching time to wean. Never use a sucking treat or pacifier. It is unnecessary and is harmful as it might excite gas in the stomach and deform the teeth."

—Dr. S. Dana Hubeard
in *Facts About Motherhood*, 1922

"Prevailing hospital conventions in our present culture require that baby should spend nearly all of this fortnight in the nursery dormitory. The nurse is permitted to bring the baby to the mother from time to time and is also permitted to hold him up behind the plate glass for inspection."

—Dr. Arnold Gesell and Dr. Frances L. Ilg
in *Infant and Child in the Culture of Today*, 1943

What would that sort of dangerous rhetoric do to a woman who wants desperately to breastfeed but for whatever reason can't? Or a woman whose child struggles to latch or reacts poorly to the breast? How about the mother who simply chooses not to breastfeed? How does that admonishment make her feel? I wanted to tell this woman exactly what I thought of her. I wanted to tell her that I was rational enough to see what she was doing (bullying a bunch of pregnant women) and that I wouldn't let her toxicity seep into my head.

But I didn't. A part of me was petrified she was right. Instead of telling her how unnecessarily cruel she was being, I decided to pull out my nipple so she could tell me what size breast pump suction cup I would need. I was a sheep.

Since the beginning of civilization, people have propagated the false narrative that motherhood is an intrinsic ability woven into the souls of all women. As expectant mothers, we are set up to believe that our "maternal instinct"—along with an abundant stream of breastmilk—would begin flowing through our body the moment our child entered the world and that we'd all be swathed in a warm wave of love as Mother Nature took the wheel.

In the hours following my delivery, most of my interaction with Tallulah occurred when the lactation consultant appeared to attach the baby onto one of my nipples. Every few hours we'd try to feed, and Tallulah would do her best to latch while I fumbled her around in different holding positions (none of which felt comfortable for either of us). She attempted to suck and pull while I winced in pain.

In between feedings, the nurses suggested I rub lanolin cream on my nipples, but applying the thick, goopy substance was like trying to spread cold butter on soft bread. Eventually, the nurse offered me those plastic turtle shells to spare my chapped, cracked, and broken boobs the torture of rubbing against my cotton nursing bra.

By the second day, all hell had broken loose. Tallulah refused to stop screaming. The nurses couldn't even do much to calm her; at one point, three different nurses, including the charge nurse, gathered in our room to try to quiet her. We didn't realize the obvious: she was starving! Or maybe they all realized, but just didn't tell me.

I had heard that babies were born with full stomachs, which is why they are usually calm, quiet, and sleepy that first day. What I didn't know was that by the second day, their stomachs were empty, but the mother's milk most likely had not come in yet. It's a really great trick Mother Nature likes to play. For me, my milk didn't come in sufficiently until day four, so Tallulah was getting only the little amount of colostrum leaking from my breasts during that swing, and she cried and fussed from hunger. And because the "breast is best" philosophy is so rampant, the nurses never even offered me the option of supplementing. Tallulah was a big baby, so her weight loss over those first days wasn't significant enough to be considered a medical risk. The nurses decided, without consulting me, that waiting for my milk to come in was what was best for my child.

Looking back, I can't help but be pissed. How dare they make that decision without offering me options! Tallulah was hungry and so uncomfortable; her cries only added to an already stressful situation (which everyone knows is not good for a new mother).

Without getting into the nitty-gritty of medical politics, many hospitals participate in the Baby-Friendly Hospital Initiative. To be considered "baby friendly," nurses are told to promote exclusive breastfeeding unless other feeding methods are deemed medically necessary.

But don't just take my word for it. This comes directly from a University of California hospital's (an accredited Baby-Friendly hospital) policies and procedures manual:

> Staff will actively support breastfeeding as the preferred method of providing nutrition to infants. . . . Mothers will be protected from the promotion of breast milk substitutes.

If a baby is not latching or a mother is not producing, the staff is then instructed to begin expressing the mother's milk by hand and spoon-feeding the infant whatever is collected. After forty-eight hours of what sounds like agonizing stress, if the baby is still not able to feed, the hospital then allows the mother to start using an electronic pump every three hours. Most importantly, the policies reassert that "mothers will be encouraged to exclusively breastfeed unless medically contraindicated" and—wait for this—"if a mother requests her infant be supplemented, staff will explore and address the mother's concerns. The mother will be taught the possible negative consequences of feeding an infant breastmilk substitutes."

I'm not saying this is all bad; I just think new mothers should have all the information. I'm sure not every hospital is this strict, and California definitely has a reputation for being a bit crunchier than other states, but it's still pretty interesting, right? The policies are clear: unless it's medically necessary, nurses are to fervently encourage every new mother to breastfeed.

Encourage is a funny word. To some, that might feel like support, guidance, and even well-intended cheerleading. However, in application "encouragement" may not always feel so warm and cozy to a new mom. In fact, it might feel like she's being pressured, bullied, or looked down on.

Look, I know the goal is to support new moms in reaching their baby-feeding goals and to provide a healthy environment for the child, and I'm all about that. I just think it's important for mamas to remember that certain hospitals might have an agenda. For example, being accredited as "baby friendly" is quite prestigious within the medical community, and having prestige is good for any business, because with that prestige often come honors, awards, funding, and donations. I can't prove that there is a *direct* link between this initiative and financial benefits to the hospital, so, legally, I can't make that argument. But, like I said, it's just something to consider.

Wow, did I get off track or what? So, back to Tallulah. By the time we got home from the hospital, my modest B cups had transformed into honeydews. Despite all the pain I was experiencing as a result of breastfeeding, I had an ample milk supply. I was in the rare category of mamas known as "overproducers" but, even so, I was still worried that I would eventually run dry. Maybe I was just experiencing some breastfeeding beginner's luck and my milk supply would soon plummet. The nurses recommended that to keep up healthy milk production I should continue to eat frequent small and healthy meals.

That's great advice, in theory.

I had a human head attached to my breast at all hours of the day. When the hell was I supposed to have time to prepare myself five to six healthy meals each day? When? WHEN? *WHEN?* When I did find a few minutes of spare time, I spent it trying to relieve yet another nipple blister with a sterilized safety pin (which I did once with a lighter in a gas station bathroom) or applying warm compresses to my boobs to help loosen up clogged milk ducts.

Some baby books suggest that you use the time after baby's first feeding of the day to pump so that you could begin storing milk. Were they joking?

Imagine if that were actually possible. I would feed my perfect little baby and she would immediately drift off into a sound slumber for the next two hours so I could shower, make a cup of coffee, eat a well-balanced meal, check my email, throw in a load of laundry, pump, and then prop my feet up and tune in to *Good Morning America* before she woke up. Right. Newborn life never goes to plan, so why do these outside voices and experts always assume that it will?

During those early days, I was astonished by all the time it consumed. Even when I was capable of breaking away for an hour, my life still revolved around my boobs. Taking a warm shower often led to a leak springing mid-shampoo, and accidentally grinding breast pump parts up in the garbage disposal caused me to take unexpected trips to buybuy Baby.

My entire schedule depended on my boobs (which no longer actually looked like my boobs): when I needed to feed, when I needed to pump, and how long I could spare in between to fit in other parts of my life. (I brought my breast pump to Neiman Marcus in Beverly Hills for the day-after-Thanksgiving sale and pumped in the third-floor dressing rooms.)

Don't get me wrong, I had no intention of stopping breastfeeding—after all, that instructor's words were seared into my brain—but I just wanted the right to bitch about it.

For the record, these are the rambling frustrations of a mama who *could* produce. Breastfeeding is really, really hard even when milk comes easy for a mom! Imagine just how hellish days could be if a mom spent endless hours pumping in the hopes of banking an ounce or two. Or if, despite all her best efforts, a mom could not get her child to latch. You become a slave to the process because you have been browbeaten into thinking that you're a shit mom if you don't subscribe to breastfeeding boot camp.

MOM-TO-MOM BREASTFEEDING TIPS

- Do some prep work. Whether that means reading a book, taking a class at your hospital, or finding an online course, educating yourself will make this experience easier. Maybe not less painful, but easier. Through these resources, you'll learn all about feeding positions and how to get a good latch (pro tip: flatten your boob between your forefinger and thumb, and shove your entire nipple into your baby's mouth like a hamburger).
- When you're in the hospital, call for a nurse or the lactation consultant *every time* you feed. Don't be shy! That's what they're there for.
- Talk to your doctor about lactation services. Whether it's an in-person consult at the hospital, a new moms' breastfeeding support group, or an in-home visit from a private lactation specialist, there are lots of options to get you the help you need.

- Suggested breastfeeding gear: the My Brest Friend nursing pillow (it's worth it, trust me); Motherlove nipple cream; a hands-free pumping bra and a car charger adapter; a Haakaa pump; breast pads; Medela Soft-Shells; Legendairy Milk lactation support supplements.
- Don't diet. It's challenging because after forty weeks of pregnancy we often feel so anxious to get our bodies back. But if you're not eating enough, your milk supply will suffer. I always had a really great supply after a couple slices of cheese pizza.
- When it comes to drinking while nursing, the general rule of thumb is this: if you shouldn't drive a car, you shouldn't nurse your baby.
- Understand that it can take about six weeks for you and your baby to get the hang of it and for your milk supply to become established.
- Allow yourself the flexibility and the grace to decide whether it is or isn't working for you.

* * *

It must be said that for some women breastfeeding isn't a chore; they are willing to put in the work without complaint. They enjoy the bond it creates and relish the beautiful relationship. They take the pills that promise to promote milk production; they make homemade oat water; they meet with experts and consultants to ensure an optimal latch . . . and sometimes it still doesn't work. That's a loss for those mamas; grieving a lost breastfeeding journey is real.

Because I was an overproducer and have fibrous breast tissue (who knew?), I was susceptible to repeated bouts of mastitis. The first case was debilitating, but with my strong supply, I knew I could recover. When mastitis returned a short time later, I knew I was on borrowed time.

So, just as George Bailey realized all the wonderful blessings in his life, and Clarence, his guardian angel, finally got his wings, I agreed to take the medication.

Between the antibiotics and the general stress of it all, my milk was gone by Christmas.

Bah humbug.

Despite not being a big fan of breastfeeding, I never imagined stopping wouldn't be on my terms. Losing my milk was yet another magical part of motherhood that fell beyond my control; I didn't have the strength within to spend days and weeks rebuilding my once fruitful supply. I'll never forget the last time I fed Tallulah. I was already dry, I knew it, but I let her attempt to feed anyway. She basically used me as a human pacifier to calm herself as we bounced on an exercise ball in her room. Tears poured down my face because I knew I'd be unable to feed her from my body again, and feelings of failure accompanied my pain (and would only be heightened by the judgmental glares of strangers that soon followed when I had the audacity to bottle-feed in public).

It wasn't until I had experienced breastfeeding myself that I truly realized how emotional it could be. Sure, I knew moms who felt brokenhearted and disappointed when the challenges began to mount, but I never really understood that emotional toll until it happened to me. I guess part of me started to fear that if I couldn't breastfeed her anymore, would she still know I was her mom? Would she still need me more than anyone else? (By the way, the answer to both is a resounding YES.)

Tallulah was eight weeks old the first time she drank formula. I couldn't be the one to give it to her; I actually had to leave the house altogether. I was incapable of feeding her on my own anymore, and I was heartbroken.

Okay. Let's stop right here for a moment.

What was happening to me? Wasn't I the same woman who sat in that plastic folding chair and scoffed at the pretentious, gratuitous lactation wizard who made shitty jokes about people's names? The same woman who saw that this instructor was feeding on the insecurities of expectant moms by insinuating that they would be harming their child if they chose to formula feed? It was absolutely crazy, because I knew better. I knew that the formula I chose for her was healthy and safe and would provide all these amazing nutrients to her still developing body and mind. I was formula fed and turned out pretty decent.

Somewhere along the line, I bought into the hype. Once I met my precious baby girl and experienced that "holy shit!" feeling of what it really means to love someone beyond all measure, the stakes got much higher. If there was even a whisper, a rumor, a theory that formula could somehow harm her, I wanted to avoid it at all costs. So, when I finally surrendered my breastfeeding journey, I couldn't help but feel like I was a massive mama failure because some woman in some classroom lit a match that I allowed to grow into a forest fire.

Somewhere during that process, the logical part of my brain had vanished. What was left was a woman with a depleted milk supply to match her depleted spirit.

I think back to the other women who paid to sit in that backroom breastfeeding seminar to learn how to do something that women have been doing since the beginning of humankind. Each knew how beneficial breastfeeding could be even before the instructor opened her big, mom-shaming mouth. That's why they paid good money to be there! And at some point after their babies arrived, when some of those women hit their breastfeeding brick walls and were forced to make a difficult decision, it was probably that woman's judgmental, terrorizing words that rang in their ears, like they did in my head.

At the end of the day, we all want to be the best mothers we can be, but only *you*—not me, and certainly not some woman in a Hollywood strip mall—know what will make you the best mom you can be and what is working against you. You're spending your free time reading this book because you want to be good for your family and yourself, which means you're already fucking crushing the mom game. Showing up and caring is 90 percent of parenting, and no kid ever turned into a serial killer because his mother chose Plum Organics formula over breastfeeding. I guarantee your child will have a hundred different things to tell a shrink, but not a single one will be, "Well, for starters, I was formula fed."

A LIST OF COMMON BREASTFEEDING CHALLENGES SO YOU CAN QUIT BEING SO HARD ON YOURSELF

Breastfeeding is hard, and it's made even more difficult when a new mama feels like it isn't coming naturally to her. I wish every mama the easiest, healthiest, and happiest breastfeeding journey (if that's what she chooses), but that's not going to be the case for most of us. It's important for mamas to remember that there is a laundry list of shit that can and will go wrong. Most nursing moms experience at least some of these challenges to breastfeeding:

- Chapped or cracked nipples
- Low milk supply
- Oversupply
- Engorgement
- Tongue tie
- Reflux
- Milk intolerance
- D-MER (dysphoric milk ejection reflex)
- Clogged ducts
- Thrush
- Mastitis
- Inverted nipples
- Trouble latching or painful latch

After my baby began drinking a wonderful lactose-free formula, guess what happened? She remained perfectly healthy and, in fact, turned into a much happier baby because not only was she fed, but also she was free of indigestion. (Like many babies, Tallulah had a lactose intolerance for the first eighteen months of her life, but I couldn't recognize it with all the other chaos going on in my home, and in my head.) Tallulah is now in preschool and has not suffered from any of those ailments that are said to befall formula-fed kids. She's just as smart as the other kids in her class, she doesn't have any known allergies, and, knock on wood, she very rarely gets sick. Look, I'm not an idiot. I understand the benefits of breastfeeding, but my question has always been: At what cost? Who is to say what is right for another family? Are you in that home? Because I'm not in yours, so I will not tell you how to handle your family business.

It poses a larger question about all the conversations about breastfeeding we're having as a culture and whether they're benefiting us or damaging us.

We've come to a point of diminishing returns. The benefit of encouraging breastfeeding above all else is no longer worth it if we're creating open season on formula-feeding moms. It's not worth it if it causes a new mom, who probably already struggles with guilt, to feel like a total failure. And it's definitely not worth it if it gives total strangers license to comment on the decisions we make, as women, about our own bodies.

To the instructors out there who spout charged judgment: You are no longer doing any good for the newborn children of America. You're just being an asshole to women who came to you looking for guidance and support.

To the many women—not all, not even most, but many—who hear these charged words and blanket judgments, and then feel inclined to regurgitate them on playgrounds, in coffee shops, and at mommy and me classes: It's simply not okay.

What's worse? Those militant experts and mamas who force "breast is best" down the throat of every expecting woman may just be their own worst enemy.

I didn't supplement with Tallulah and breastfed for only eight weeks. Maybe if I had the luxury of supplementing on occasion, I wouldn't have felt so much pressure. Maybe I would have recognized her lactose intolerance and adjusted my diet accordingly. Maybe being able to supplement a feed so that I could go for a walk would have given me the mental health break I needed to push forward with my journey.

I supplemented with my son on the second day of his life (much to the dismay of a very judgmental nurse who told me that she couldn't "really recommend it") and continued to offer him one formula feed for the first two weeks, after which I exclusively breastfed until he was six months old.

Am I absolutely certain there's a connection? No.

But what I do know, with no uncertainty, is that one of the most important things in a new family is a healthy, happy baby . . . and mama. By whatever means necessary.

10 WHEN A GOOD CRY BECOMES A TSUNAMI

"Just get outside and go for a walk," my husband suggested, throwing on his jacket before heading out the door to begin what I not-so-fondly referred to as his "nine-hour vacation" . . . or, work.

Monday mornings were always the hardest. Starting on Sunday evening, I would begin to dread the week ahead: five full days of solitary time at home. My husband would head off to work in the morning, and I would be alone with my baby for the next ten hours. Most likely, Tallulah and I would take turns crying and eating; if she happened to sleep, I would end up doing laundry or cleaning dishes. I'd watch a few episodes of *Sons of Anarchy* while she ate; eventually, I would dig through the freezer until I found something I could heat up for dinner. If I was lucky, she'd take a second nap and I could squeeze in a shower and brush my teeth. Otherwise, I'd spend a good portion of the day swaddling, re-swaddling, and re-swaddling again before finally giving up.

"I think the fresh air would do you good," he said, before adding, "and it might feel good to get some exercise."

I paused for a beat before responding.

"Did you just call me fat?" I asked, in a voice so calm it even made me nervous.

He just looked at me. I assume he was replaying what he had just said and trying to figure out how the hell I made that leap.

"Do you want me to go walking because you're sick of looking at me in my fat girl jeans?" I said, my voice getting louder. "You know that our daughter hates the stroller and hates being in a wrap, so how would you suggest I take her for a walk? Don't you think I would if I could? Do you think I want to look this way?"

"Leslie," he started, eyes gaping. "I just thought that getting out of the house for a little bit might help you feel better. That's all."

I wasn't even listening by that point and decided to surrender to the hot tears rolling down my cheeks. To be honest, I'm not completely sure what I was crying about: the assumed commentary on my weight or the idea of starting another week alone with our newborn. Probably both. Probably neither. Or maybe I was just desperate for his attention and compassion.

"Babe," he tried again, softer this time. "I only thought that getting out in the sunshine would be good for your spirits. That's all."

He had the best intentions, I knew that, but it was almost easier to make excuses or to admit defeat before even trying than it was to yet again feel the disappointment of something else blowing up in my face. I avoided trying anything new, because I didn't want to experience the guilt of failure. I looked at my daughter's sweet, beautiful little face and couldn't help but feel sorry for her. She got saddled with this sad sack of a mom who couldn't seem to figure it out.

I nodded and promised him I would give it a try before allowing him to step foot out the door and begin his day. To his credit, it was finally beginning to feel like fall in Los Angeles and maybe Tallulah would enjoy the crisp, cool air on her little face.

It was after lunchtime when I managed to put on my sneakers. I bundled Tallulah up in a little fleece and tucked her into a cotton baby wrap that my friend had given us, promising it would be my saving grace. I snapped headphones in my ears and started out the door, determined to make this outing a success: a nice little stroll up our rolling canyon street. The fresh air would be good for both of us, and I could have a small victory to tell my husband about that night.

Roughly three minutes into our walk (approximately one Adele song), Tallulah started to fuss. I shushed and patted her bottom and tried to cover her head with a receiving blanket to block her face from the sun and breeze, but I could feel her small body continue to wiggle around. Simultaneously, I could feel my own muscles tense and my jaw clench. She was on her way to a total meltdown, and my body was preparing itself for the storm.

Everything that I tried to do for her she seemed to hate, which was why my days and weeks were just a blur of the only two things that seemed to make her happy: eating and bouncing, eating and bouncing. I tried, I really tried, but I couldn't figure out how to make her like those smiley, cooing, bubbly little babies I'd see on Facebook, Instagram, and television.

(To this day, I'm not sure why Tallulah fought so hard against the things that were intended to bring her comfort. Maybe it was constant stomachaches? Maybe she was just so overtired? Maybe she was preparing me for what it's going to be like when she gets to high school? I wanted desperately to be a source of comfort for her, and little did I know then that for the rest of her life, I would be . . . and she would be mine.)

I couldn't even go on a ten-minute walk. It felt like I spent more time crying than I did celebrating, which only made me cry harder. That couldn't be normal! I knew something wasn't right, but

I was buried so deep in trying to figure out how to be a mom that I couldn't see it.

Determined to do something for myself, I pressed forward . . . and so did she. The farther we walked, the harder she cried. I decided she was testing my willpower and that eventually one of us would break. I started to bargain with myself:

She'd fall asleep soon. She couldn't keep this up forever.

But I knew she could. I knew just how strong-willed my daughter was, even as an infant.

I thought back to those early days in the hospital. When the nurses asked me to fill out a postpartum evaluation form before discharge, I remember thinking how ridiculous all the prompts sounded:

"I have been unable to laugh or see the funny side of things: always, sometimes, on occasion, not often, never" and "I have blamed myself unnecessarily when things went wrong: always, sometimes, on occasion, not often, never," and so on.

"Are they kidding me with this?" I had asked my husband. "I had the baby, like, five minutes ago."

"Just fill it out," he said. We had spent the past three days stuffed into a ten-by-ten room on the maternity floor of Cedars-Sinai. Although this particular hospital was known for its luxury accommodations for VIP patients, I was definitely not getting the celebrity treatment.

The questions felt a bit premature. It's like they were asking me to predict the future; I hadn't even left the hospital yet. Didn't I need to actually experience motherhood before filling out a form on whether or not it was driving me over the edge? But I was anxious to get going, so I completed the survey and handed it over. Given my new mama excitement and the fact that I had yet to experience the true scope of sleep deprivation, I passed with flying colors (surprise, surprise).

If I were to take that same test the day we went for a walk, I would not have done as well.

I turned the volume up on my iPhone to drown out Tallulah's crying as my own tears rolled down my face for probably the fifth time since breakfast. I was trapped, and resentful and anxious. Everyone around me told me the newborn period was just a phase, that things would get easier, but I couldn't see the light at the end of the tunnel. I was in the middle of the shit storm, and my future looked bleak.

"Think of it this way, Leslie," my mother had said. "She's six weeks old now. You're halfway through the hardest part."

She really thought this would make me feel better.

"Six more weeks," I sobbed. "How am I supposed to do this for six more weeks?" It felt never-ending.

I kept walking up the street. We both might as well just sink into our misery.

"Leslie!" a familiar voice shouted. I pulled an earbud out and spun around to see my neighbor approaching.

"Hi," I said, quickly brushing the tears off my cheeks.

"How's it going?" she asked, bounding toward me, a yoga mat tucked under her arm. She was roughly my age, a tried-and-true canyon hippie. She and her boyfriend welcomed a little boy into the world about six months before Tallulah. My husband often joked that we liked the idea of having this couple as friends, because they checked all the compatibility boxes, but neither side ever took the steps toward advancing a friendship. We had been cordial neighbors for the past four years, and that was how it was destined to remain.

"Great," I lied.

I watched as she scanned my face, seeming to register with one glance what was going on. She sighed and her shoulders fell. My entire body tightened. I felt like such a loser as it was; I didn't want her sympathy on top of it all. I didn't want anyone to know how badly I was fumbling it all, especially a girl in a crop top.

"It gets easier," she offered.

I had so much snot running out of my nose that I went to laugh but instead some sort of offensive-sounding chortle escaped me.

"Seriously," she continued. "I know it can feel like it never will, but it does." I know she wanted to be there for me, but given our nonfriendship relationship, I could tell she wasn't sure what would be considered overstepping on a new mom during this very sensitive time.

I didn't say anything but decided to let the tears fall freely from under my sunglasses.

"It's okay to feel sad," she said, rubbing the side of my arm.

"It is?" I asked.

"Yes," she replied. We stood in silence for a second, before I muttered something about having to get back to the house.

"Hang in there, girl," she said, before turning toward her garage.

Looking back, I'm certain she recognized something in me at the time that I had trouble seeing myself: I was suffering.

SHIT YOU SHOULD KNOW: WHAT ARE PERINATAL MOOD AND ANXIETY DISORDERS?

Consider this your PMAD 101 course. By no means does this list cover every possibility, but it is meant to offer new moms (and partners and friends) insight into what they may be experiencing.

Postpartum depression: The hallmarks include the inability to enjoy moments worth enjoying and difficulty bonding with your baby as well as excessive crying, withdrawing from loved ones, and increased anger and disconnect.

Postpartum anxiety (can include **postpartum social anxiety disorder** and **postpartum generalized anxiety disorder):** Mothers live in a state of hypervigilance, fear, and irritability. A woman with an anxiety disorder is unable to turn off thoughts of harm even when things are fine. The anxiety is constant; they can't stop the stream of thoughts. An example is lying awake at night obsessing about how something you did or did not do could negatively impact the baby.

Postpartum panic disorder: Frequent or occasional panic attacks caused largely by fears of harm coming to the baby. This particular disorder is most often triggered by an event and therefore is usually an offshoot of a postpartum anxiety disorder or postpartum PTSD.

Postpartum OCD (obsessive-compulsive disorder): A variation of postpartum anxiety in which a mother experiences intrusive thoughts that can be violent, sexual, or even totally outlandish. For instance, if you throw out every knife in your kitchen because you're afraid it might jump into your hand and force you to harm the baby. These thoughts come over and over again, and you are unable to shut them off.

Postpartum PTSD (post-traumatic stress disorder): This includes reexperiencing a *perceived* trauma (something medically wrong may not have happened, but the mother relives it as such) that causes you to have flashbacks and nightmares of the traumatic event. The key here is the anxiety it causes toward the new baby. Without treatment, you can't talk yourself out of it.

Postpartum psychosis (a variant of **postpartum bipolar disorder):** People suffering from postpartum bipolar disorder don't sleep, but they appear very energetic. They speak very quickly, but don't make a lot of sense. This can translate quickly into psychosis, the most severe of the PMADs, in which mothers have delusions, auditory hallucinations, and visual hallucinations. Psychosis is considered a medical emergency but not a woman's fault. There is a legitimate risk of harm to the woman and the child. Psychosis occurs in one to two postpartum women out of a thousand.

I had more challenging days than good ones. I spent much of the time crying, over nothing and everything. I didn't respond to logic or reason. I was wallowing in a phase I must have known could only be temporary. I was riddled with anxiety and resentment. I was sad so much of the time, and that made me feel like such an asshole. I wanted to be happy but couldn't keep the sadness from seeping into my daily life. And because I wasn't chronically overjoyed all the time, I started to feel guilty. Bringing a new little person into the world was such a blessing, and I felt like a horrible human for not loving every minute.

How is it that I was flooded with information on which stroller to get, which detergent to use, and which breast pump to buy, but no one ever thought to offer any information on postpartum depression or any other perinatal mood and anxiety disorder (PMAD)? Statistics show that approximately one out of five women suffers from a disorder associated with the postpartum period, but we're completely left in the dark about what these are, how they look, and what we should do.

It's not just negligent, it's dangerous!

I was always made to feel that it was one way or the other: either you're a happy, well-adjusted mama or you're wanting to cause physical harm to yourself or your child. I went to the end of the internet researching baby formula, but I never thought to google "symptoms of postpartum depression."

I could write an entire book on how our healthcare system fails to meet the needs of postpartum mothers—even though I have nothing but respect for my team of doctors who helped me through delivering two children. I didn't just need an ob-gyn; I needed a nutritionist, a pelvic floor therapist, a psychologist, and a medically trained postpartum doula. I needed a village.

Luckily, our society is finally recognizing these gaping holes and is doing its best to keep up with the demands of the modern mother. A decade ago, a woman was made to feel incredible shame if she admitted to having symptoms of depression after her baby was born. We saw it play out on the Hollywood stage in 2005 when Brooke Shields took Tom Cruise to task when he suggested her postpartum depression wasn't a real thing, and her mood could simply be cured with vitamins and exercise. The culture has come a long way, but there is still much work to be done.

For starters, women need to get educated! Being the research junkie I am how the hell, in 2014, did I not know that I had a 20 percent chance of developing postpartum depression? Are we afraid that women are too fragile or precious to handle real talk? We push humans out of our vaginas; I think I can manage to swallow some statistics—no matter how startling—on how our minds might react to this massive life event.

In writing this book, I connected with postpartum specialists Paige Bellenbaum and Dr. Catherine Birndorf of the Motherhood Center in New York—a practice that offers support services to new and expecting mothers and provides treatment options for women suffering from a wide range of perinatal mood and anxiety disorders—as well as Dr. Carly Snyder, attending physician in the Department of Psychiatry at Mount Sinai Beth Israel and a President's Advisory Council member for Postpartum Support International. Because I'm not a medical professional (although I have diagnosed many rare, incurable ailments in myself and my family via WebMD), I thought it was important to offer some advice from people who actually know their shit.

Many professionals on the front lines of advancing postpartum wellness are starting to shy away from the term *postpartum depression*. The term is limiting, unable to distinguish among the many mood disorders a woman could experience as a result of her pregnancy and childbirth and too narrowly specifying the period when she might experience them.

They are moving toward broader terminology to ensure women who are suffering aren't overlooked because they can't directly relate to the key terms *postpartum* and *depression*. The idea is that women can easily experience a mood disorder at any stage of the reproductive process, and for many women that includes the time before pregnancy when they are trying to conceive—a stressful period for many families—and, of course, during the course of the pregnancy itself.

It's ironic that just as we as a culture become comfortable talking about postpartum depression, we go and change up all the medical jargon to really confuse the shit out of people. But if they're changing it in a way that can help more of us figure out what the fuck is happening in our early days of motherhood, I'm on board. Far too often women are left to suffer alone because what they're experiencing doesn't fall squarely into that "postpartum depression" box.

The term *perinatal mood and anxiety disorders* is much more inclusive.

Perinatal means "before, after, and during pregnancy." The addition of the word *anxiety* addresses the fact that some experts believe more women today suffer from anxiety than depression (a very buzzy topic of conversation in many mama Facebook groups). A new mom may be suffering, but if she's not experiencing the hallmark traits of depression, she may not realize that she needs to get help. Postpartum depression is one of the main disorders in this category; it's just not the *only* one.

More and more women are experiencing anxiety as related to their pregnancy and postpartum period, and although it manifests differently from how depression manifests and often with opposite symptoms, it still falls in the same category as depression and is often treated in a similar way. For example, an anxious mom might not be able to sleep because she is overwhelmed with fear that her baby might stop breathing, whereas a depressed mom might not feel the desire to get out of bed to care for her baby. An anxious mom might not allow another to care for her baby, whereas a depressed mom might feel ambivalence toward her child.

Despite the conversations we're now having about perinatal wellness, postpartum depression and many of the perinatal mood and anxiety disorders are still shrouded in mystery. To begin with, most women just aren't well educated on the topic. I wasn't, and my business is all about early motherhood!

There is a lot of misinformation out there, and, at the same time, there isn't a lot of solid, dependable information, either, because postpartum depression isn't well understood yet, even after all these years.

Here's the thing that really surprised me: I always thought postpartum depression was triggered by a specific physiological occurrence during pregnancy or labor and delivery, but, really, postpartum depression is basically plain old depression that occurs during a finite window of time (the first year of your child's life). Dr. Birndorf admits that postpartum depression does look and feel a bit different from standard depression because the people suffering from it just underwent a huge life event, so it tends to be a more anxious experience, although it is diagnosed and treated in the same way as depression.

Additionally, many questions women ask about the disorder can be answered in the exact same way as they are answered for depression.

If I didn't experience PPD with my first, can I develop it with my second?

Yes, because it's a form of depression, and depression can happen to anyone at any time.

I had my baby via C-section. Can I still get PPD?

Yes, because it's just a form of depression, and not conditional on how you deliver.

My baby is already ten months old. Can I develop PPD now?

Yes, because it's just depression, and depression can occur at any time. It's considered postpartum depression up to twelve months after delivery.

Can my husband get PPD?

Is your husband a breathing human? Then, yes, he can develop depression like anyone else.

"Everyone is quick to blame hormones [for PPD], and I'm the first to jump on the bandwagon if it makes people feel better, but the truth is, we don't really know what causes it," Birndorf says. "And it frustrates me to say that, because of course there's some connection, right? It seems so obvious, but we just don't have the evidence yet."

She acknowledges that the crazy shift in hormones—when estrogen and progesterone surge before birth and plummet a few days after delivery—can and does trigger the baby blues, but that's a separate condition.

Baby blues most typically occur in the two-week period after delivering; the symptoms women experience are hyperemotionality and hypersensitivity. Think: "I don't even know why I'm crying!" type of stuff. However, because it is caused by the hormone imbalance, there is a clear cutoff when our sadness, anxiety, and having ALL THE FEELINGS can no longer be considered "baby blues." I'm throwing a lot at you right now, I know, but it's important for women to understand!

Birndorf does not rule out that hormones in some way play a part in the large number of women experiencing perinatal mood and anxiety disorders, she just says it's not the whole story and doesn't want people to ignore a larger issue.

"To me, I believe it has more to do with a psychological shift, an identity shift," she says. "It's a life stage that we do not acknowledge. It's not like you pop a kid out and say, 'I'm a mother now. I know how to do this!' Of course you don't know what you're doing. And why should you? You've never done this before. It doesn't always come naturally or easily. It's a developmental stage that requires development!"

(Since writing this book, the term "matrescence" has sprung up more and more among experts when describing the transition into motherhood and how it closely resembles adolescence in terms of development, hormone adjustment, and so on. I highly recommend you google the TED talk by Alexandra Sacks. It's eye-opening AF.)

I wanted to know more about the *why*. Yes, we are all susceptible to depression at any point, but what about early motherhood makes it occur much more commonly?

"Social factors are very important, but sleep deprivation is huge," says Dr. Carly Snyder. "If you're not sleeping, all bets are off. Sleep deprivation is used at Guantanamo as a form of torture, because *it is* torture!"

Because the days, weeks, and months after having a child are often so intense, it's easy to overlook symptoms of postpartum depression or anxiety and to write off any overwhelming or scary feelings as those "pesky hormones." More often than not, women go undiagnosed and, even worse, untreated. Unfortunately, there isn't a blood test to determine whether or not you have developed a perinatal mood and anxiety disorder; you might have just breezed through a postpartum wellness survey, checking all the boxes you knew would make you pass. So, as if a new mom didn't have enough going on already, she needs to be responsible for staying on top of her mental health and recognizing when things go off the tracks.

"Pregnant women and postpartum women are very big on talking about how hard it all is, almost as a badge of honor," says Dr. Snyder. "But you should *not* feel like you're drowning and you can't find a lifeline."

Dr. Birndorf says that awareness is key and that all expecting moms should educate themselves and their closest companions to help spot any signs or symptoms of a developing condition. "You're in the worst shape of your life, so it's unfair that you have to be accountable for it, but it takes a village. The most important thing is to just be truthful and not pretend," she says. "And don't let anyone tell you you're fine when you know you're not."

The two things new moms and those closest to them should be looking for are the length of time a woman experiences these feelings and how much it affects her life.

Because there is no standard course for medically responding to a PMAD, it can be really scary for us to admit that we need help. The good news is that once a woman finds a healthcare provider she feels comfortable speaking to, she has options on how to treat.

"No one can put a pill in your mouth," Dr. Birndorf says. Many moms—particularly those who are breastfeeding—fear that if they open up about what they're feeling they'll be forced to go on medication, but that is not the case. Although Birndorf emphasizes that there are plenty of perfectly safe medications that can treat PMADs during breastfeeding, no doctor is going to force you to do something you're not comfortable with. There are other routes a mom can take—even nonbreastfeeding moms who prefer to stay away from pharmaceuticals.

Self-care is one of the most important and effective ways of treating PMADs: eating well, exercising, getting enough sleep.

"When people get to me and they're like, 'how about that med?' I always say, 'First, how are you taking care of yourself?'" Birndorf says. "Because if they're drinking every night or up late every night, medication is not going to work."

Additionally, she says talk therapy is very effective in combatting PMADs. Often, it's the first step for women in recognizing what is happening within their own world. It's the first opportunity since having a baby to sit down and reflect on what this new life is all about.

"There is zero shame in women having a perinatal mood disorder," says Dr. Snyder. "This is not their fault; this is biology. If this is happening, we owe it to ourselves and our babies to get help."

If you believe that you or someone you know may be experiencing a perinatal mood or anxiety disorder, please seek treatment. Postpartum Support International is an organization dedicated to providing help and assistance to families suffering from postpartum depression, anxiety, and other mood disorders. It can help women find resources and support locally as well as through PSI programs.

Call 1-800-944-4773 or email support@postpartum.net.

Regardless of what you feel you may or may not be experiencing, the most important thing that all new moms should know is this: you are not alone.

11 NOT SLEEPING IS THE ENEMY: TOOLS FOR SAVING YOUR SANITY

"We're not changing our entire life for the baby."

Like countless mothers before me, I, too, uttered these famous last words.

Prior to our daughter being born, I was convinced that adding a new baby to our family meant that she would simply adapt to the life my husband and I chose to live; it just came down to parenting. We'd be like one of those crunchy, go-with-the-flow couples you see in Old Navy commercials. We'd tote her along to dinner parties and spend lazy weekend afternoons at the beach because our baby would, of course, be oh-so-mellow. On a whim, we'd probably decide to travel to Cambodia with our six-month-old (because it was about time she started seeing the world). For the record, I grew up on the McDonald's Happy Meal, but something about becoming a mother caused me to become crunchy as fuck. I would research every piece of "on-the-go" baby merch available, which my child was guaranteed to love (I mean, the baby on the box sure looked happy!). We'd fold her into our existing life; we didn't need to reinvent the wheel.

Look, I wasn't completely oblivious to the realities of starting a family. I had already traded in my two-seat convertible for a more practical soccer mom mobile, and even swapped out our glass coffee table for a pair of cushioned foot stools. It's just that my husband and I decided early on that if we allowed the baby to rule our world, we were doomed. You see, given the chance, babies are remarkable magicians. Once they arrive, *poof*, a person's entire pre-baby life disappears: the things they used to value bend to the needs of their child before eventually fading away entirely.

My husband and I—as ignorant as we were arrogant—chalked up this "disappearing act" to other parents being unable to manage their new existence. They collapsed under the pressure of a new baby instead of rising to the occasion. Given all the time I spent preparing for Tallulah to join our family, I couldn't imagine her having any cause for complaint, and, therefore, she'd be an easy baby to care for. After all, it's our responsibility to teach our children to be flexible and adaptable. At least, that's how *we* intended to parent.

Was I worried about her routine? Lord, no. She was going to be the kind of baby who could sleep anywhere. I'd strap her into an organic cloth baby carrier (with five-star reviews), and off we'd go. After all, babies sleep. That's what they do. Right?

Wrong. So very, very wrong.

I'm the first to admit that prior to having a baby I was a selfish ass. For thirty-two years, I had the luxury of having to worry about only myself and, on occasion, my husband (who, for the most part, was pretty self-reliant). Besides the standard commitments of job, family, and the general rule of law, I was able to live my life however I chose to live it and I balked at the idea of giving up that freedom.

I could decide to go to the movies on a random Wednesday night and pop into a spin class on a Saturday afternoon. After work, I could catch up on phone calls with girlfriends or meet my husband for dinner at our favorite Mexican restaurant. I woke up at ten on the weekends and planned last-minute weekend road trips because, why not? Generally speaking, my life was, well, mine . . . not to mention pretty damn amazing. Through school and career, I had worked my ass off to create this existence for myself. Don't get it twisted, I definitely paid my dues eating Top Ramen and living on the top bunk of a closet-sized studio without air-conditioning (or pest control), but by the time I hit my thirties, I was finally reaping the benefits. It's not everybody's reality, and I felt very fortunate to call it mine.

Albeit foolish, I was under the assumption that because my child grew in my body and she spent forty weeks absorbing everything I enjoyed, she'd continue that trend after birth. She'd like my taste in music; she'd sleep when I slept; she'd devour whatever I ate and basically adhere to my general lifestyle. Never once did it cross my mind that she would have a personality, opinions, and a digestive system of her own (at least not until she hit that "tween" stage). It's clear to me now that I was planning for a baby, not necessarily a person.

After she was born, it didn't take long for me to realize that my casual approach to living may not go exactly to plan. Tallulah had her own ideas of how our life together was going to look, and she didn't appear to have any interest in being a go-with-the-flow kind of kid. In fact, it became evident she was more of a "dig her heels into the sand and scream" sort. Not only was she incredibly alert and easily overstimulated, she also suffered from indigestion, so I spent most of my time with a cranky infant who couldn't settle and who flat out refused to sleep. Like, ever.

It's important to note that all babies are different, and it really is a crapshoot. Each baby is his or her own little person, and parents will likely learn that pretty early on. Some babies can power through stomachaches and overtiredness with a bit of whining (my son ended up being one of those magical creatures), but that was not Tallulah's personality. Our child had what early childhood development experts refer to as "big feelings."

Her feelings often became so large that there was no room for anything else in our lives, our day, and our home. My mom suggested that she might be colicky. I was a colicky baby, so it only made sense that my daughter would suffer the same malady. But how was I supposed to know the difference between colic and regular indigestion? Maybe she was just overtired? Maybe she had an invisible strand of hair wrapped around her pinky toe? Maybe she was the spawn of Satan?

I couldn't hear my own thoughts long enough to properly diagnose the situation, and I felt shackled to our house simply because "going out" was no longer worth it. Even if I could get past my own insecurities about how her sobs would affect everyone else at a restaurant, park, or store, I still couldn't manage how her crying affected me (or my mammary glands).

Nights were the loneliest hours of my life. She and I would huddle together, as I shushed, rocked, and bounced her, praying she would finally drift off for an hour or two. My head bobbled up and down as I tried to keep myself alert. I'd cry because it felt like I was the only person awake in the entire world. I was half-consumed with heartbreak and half-consumed with total exhaustion.

Weeks turned to months and I faced the harsh realization that my pre-baby life was a thing of the past. I didn't even have the time or desire to grasp at straws; it was all just slipping through my fingers. My friends with children—the ones I had foolishly judged and considered way too subservient to their own kids—had seemingly managed to find a much better balance than I could.

Without even fully recognizing it, I became everything I swore I'd never be. The parts of my life that I took for granted (like washing my face or putting on shoes) were now luxuries, and getting used to that required a major shift in my priorities.

When it came to motherhood, I was out of my element. Just when I needed self-confidence the most, I had none. I had never felt so out of control. But one thing I knew for sure: I needed to figure something out. This unhappy routine was taking a toll on my mental health, and Tallulah couldn't have been enjoying things all that much either

"You need to get her on a schedule," my friend Lindsay told me. Her son was born seven months before Tallulah and, just looking at her, it appeared she had managed the transition into motherhood seemingly well: she wore jeans, brushed her hair, and even put on lip gloss!

By this point, I had read enough books and articles to recognize that most children—even babies—don't like surprises. Small people thrive when they know what to expect and when to expect it; establishing a routine is particularly important when you have a "big feelings" kind of baby. Even though a schedule meant I was completely abandoning any last hope of being one of those "take the baby with me" kind of moms, I was finally ready to do it. The chaos approach to parenting was clearly not working. We both needed a little predictability, and we both needed sleep.

And sleep is the most critical aspect of any newborn schedule.

Every parenting book on the market tells you how significant infant sleep is. They beat you over the head with it. My issue wasn't understanding the importance of sleep; it was figuring out *how* to get my baby to fall asleep. Not one of the nine parenting books—nine!—that I had sitting on my coffee table offered an effective strategy. All they did was remind me how detrimental it was for her development that she wasn't sleeping (sleep is when blood supply to the muscles increases, when hormones that support growth are released, etc., etc.)

AN OBNOXIOUS LIST OF NEWBORN SLEEP BOOKS THAT MAY OR MAY NOT WORK

» *Cherish the First 6 Weeks*

» *Secrets of the Baby Whisperer*

» *On Becoming Babywise*

» *The Happiest Baby on the Block*

» *Twelve Hours' Sleep by Twelve Weeks Old*

» *Healthy Sleep Habits, Happy Child*

» *The 90-Minute Baby Sleep Program*

» *3 Day Sleep Solution*

» *The Baby Sleep Solution*

For weeks, I tried every damn trick in the book(s) to get her to fall asleep with ease: rocking, shushing, car seats, swaddles, wraps, strollers, swinging, infant massage, and even essential oils in her bath. Not only did none of it work, but she seemed to hate everything babies were supposed to love. I panicked thinking my baby would face serious developmental setbacks as a result of her sleeplessness . . . and it would all be my fault.(By now, you're probably noticing a common theme of self-blame, and you would be correct. Mom guilt is just another one of the joys of parenthood I was ill-prepared for. More on that in Chapter 15.) When I explained this to the pediatrician, he laughed and assured me that nothing was wrong with Tallulah and that I was just the proud parent of a very "spirited" child. ("Spirited" is something people say when they want to politely tell you that your kid is a pain in the ass. To this day, my daughter is very "spirited.")

When Tallulah was about fourteen weeks old, recognizing just how out of my depth I was, I decided to enlist the help of an infant sleep expert, Melissa Brown, a certified sleep consultant and founder of SleepShop. Sleeping, she explained, was a learned skill that my daughter had yet to master. Instead of getting her to fall asleep, I needed to teach her *how* to fall asleep. Once she learned how to fall asleep, she would no longer depend on me to do it for her. It would give my young daughter the independence she needed to thrive and afford me a bit of a break throughout the day. More importantly, once she was getting enough sleep, she'd become a happier, easier-to-manage baby because she wouldn't be constantly overtired.

Some of you may read this and recoil at the very idea of sleep training. Opinions on this particular topic are as charged as they are varied; the phrase itself has become a loaded term. Some families believe firmly in allowing their baby to cry it out, while others believe that allowing a baby to cry for an extended period of time is tantamount to torture. Some people believe in co-sleeping with their babies, while some believe that a baby should always be in his or her own crib.

I find that most families' opinions lay somewhere in the middle. The most important thing for any new family to remember is that a rested family is a happy family. As previously mentioned, sleep deprivation is largely acknowledged as the leading cause of postpartum mood disorders, so it's crucial you figure out the most effective way for everyone to get some sleep, whether that means afternoon naps on mama's chest or a graduated extinction method (check and console after set periods of time).

When we decided to get sleep help for Tallulah, it was a little earlier than typically recommended (the ideal window, according to most pediatricians, is between four and six months), but the constant fight to get her to sleep was becoming all-consuming. I didn't know how much longer I could manage it. It's also important to note that many working moms need to go back to work around the three- to four-month mark, and that requires getting enough sleep to properly function. I barely had enough reserve to brush my teeth, let alone the energy to be productive outside of what was necessary for survival. I wasn't prepared to let her scream for hours on end; I knew I needed guidance . . . for all of our sakes.

During the in-person consult, Brown confirmed my worst fears: Tallulah was a highly alert baby. In fact, she said Tallulah may have been the most challenging sleeper she had ever encountered because even the smallest disturbance kept her awake.

Immediately, Brown diagnosed one of the major issues in our sleep debacle: the nursery.

Traditionally, I'm a bit of a minimalist when it comes to décor: neutral colors and clean lines. However, during my pregnancy with Tallulah, all the added hormones really brought to the surface underlying girly tendencies, and I decided the nursery needed to be *all of the pink*.

The theme, I told my husband, was a contemporary nod to Alice in Wonderland.

"What does that even mean?" he asked. I still don't have an answer, but I painted the nursery a nausea-inducing shade of Pepto-Bismol pink, complete with an enormous mural of an English rose behind the crib. If that wasn't enough, I hung a glistening crystal chandelier in the already brightly lit room and laid out a dizzying black-and-white-striped rug to cover the entire floor.

The key to getting any child to sleep—and any adult, for that matter—is creating optimal sleeping conditions . . . how could I expect my baby to drift peacefully off to dreamland when her nursery looked like an acid trip? Immediately, Brown instructed me to order a white noise machine on Amazon and some blackout curtains from Ikea. Tallulah needed minimal outside stimuli and absolute darkness.

It was also important, Brown reminded me, that I not allow her to get overtired (which was hilarious because she was perpetually overtired), and that meant adhering to a strict routine throughout the day. Routine would also offer Tallulah cues; she'd learn that after she slept, she ate, and after she ate, she played, and after she played, she slept, and so on. She would no longer feel the need to cry in order to have her needs met (at least not as much), because there was an established routine to meet them. It would give both Tallulah and me a bit of confidence that I actually knew what the hell I was doing.

SAMPLE SCHEDULE AT FOURTEEN WEEKS

7 a.m. Wake up
7:15 a.m. Eat
8:30 a.m. Nap
10:15 a.m. Wake up
10:30 a.m. Eat
12 p.m. Nap
1:45 p.m. Wake up
2 p.m. Eat
3:30 p.m. Nap
4:45 p.m. Wake up
5 p.m. Eat
5:45 p.m. Bathe
6:15 p.m. Eat again
6:45 p.m. Bedtime

I had to be diligent about following the schedule, and knowing my daughter, Brown warned me there would be crying. To this day, I can't bear to hear my children cry. It rips at my heart now, just as it did then, so I was hesitant and anxious about the whole process.

But, to hear Brown tell it, sleep training does not promote or encourage parents and caregivers to allow the child to cry for need-based reasons (pain, hunger, etc.), though that is one misconception about it. Sleep training a baby means allowing them to acclimate to a new routine and allowing them the opportunity to discover how to calm themselves (known as "self-soothing), during which babies might cry because they're simply used to something different (like being nursed to sleep).

"Having a baby protest, whine, or be frustrated is not harmful," she says. "A baby isn't saying, 'Hey, Mom, I want to stay awake.' The baby is saying, 'Hey, Mom, you used to rock me to sleep and you're not doing that anymore. That's frustrating.'"

It's not easy or pleasant to hear your baby be upset, and it's up to the parents to decide how often they will allow it (if at all). But for those who choose to allow for some crying, it makes it easier to think about it in these terms.

Often the argument against allowing a child to fuss is the fear of increasing cortisol levels in a crying baby, but Brown reassured me that cortisol levels in an overtired baby are much higher than those of a baby who cries out of frustration before falling asleep. Like all things in newborn life, the frustration would be temporary. Once Tallulah got the hang of the whole sleep thing, there would be no more crying at nap time and bedtime, and a lot more sleeping. If I continued to allow her to be overtired, her cortisol levels would continue to be high until she started getting enough rest.

Another misconception about sleep training is that it requires you to abandon your baby, which isn't totally true. Brown assured me that I could still comfort and cuddle my baby while teaching her to sleep. My baby would still know I was there; I could tell her I love her, shush her, rub her head, and use my hand to pat her belly, but the goal was to keep her in the crib so she could learn to fall asleep independently. I should note that there are a hundred different ways you can get your baby on a schedule and sleeping more regularly; plus, not every family feels the need to follow a particular routine (and that's great, too); this is just the path we chose to follow.

For me, I needed an approach that could promise results in a gentle way but also as quickly as possible. The idea that one day I would sleep six uninterrupted hours felt like a dream! To manage my child, my life, my home, and one day soon, my work, I needed to restore some sanity to my life ASAP.

I read somewhere once (back when I had time to read) that habits can be formed or broken in a matter of three days. Brown, and most sleep-training experts, agreed that it would take roughly three days for my daughter to catch on to this new routine. Ironically, the week we decided to tackle sleep training was the week of my thirty-third birthday, and getting my child to sleep would be the ultimate gift to myself.

Much like one readies for combat, I prepared to hunker down with my baby for approximately seventy-two hours, after which one of us would emerge victorious. I sent my husband to work and locked the doors. She and I were going to battle.

SHIT YOU SHOULD KNOW: FIVE SLEEP BASICS

1. **Create a suitable sleep environment.**
   Think dark room, white noise, a cool temperature, some sort of sleep sack, and a safe bed. "The temperature is important, because a baby's body temperature rises during sleep cycles and when transitioning into sleep cycles," Melissa Brown says. "Soon the baby will start associating sleep with all these cues." True story, I ended up taping black garbage bags to the windows of Tallulah's room. From the outside, her nursery looked like a crack house.
2. **Establish a bedtime routine.**
   Example: bath, jammies, books, songs, cuddles, and bed. "This will help your baby associate going to bed as a very special time spent with you," says Brown. "It's important to keep it consistent so the baby begins to know what to expect."
3. **Relax on the naps.**
   New parents often get so stressed over their newborn's schedule, but a child's nap routine doesn't usually stabilize until six months. The most important thing is getting them well established with a bedtime routine first.

4. **Don't keep your baby up longer than he or she should be.**

   Getting your baby to sleep before he or she becomes overtired is crucial. It is less of a battle to get a tired but not overtired child to fall asleep, and sleep is important for brain development and mental rest. "When a child is up too long, their body secretes a hormone similar to adrenaline that then keeps them up even longer," Brown says. "Sometimes babies—and kids—are the most tired when they appear to be the opposite of tired." Wake windows for each baby are different, so use trial and error to figure out what works best for your little one.

5. **Some days will just suck.**

   Regardless of how strictly you follow the schedule and routine, some days are just going to throw you a curve ball. "They're not robots, they're tiny humans. Some days they're just not going to find their groove," Brown says. You also have to give yourself the grace to divert from the routine when necessary and accept the repercussions (e.g., skipping a nap to pick someone up from the airport, or hitting traffic and being late for the bedtime routine). The important thing is not to let one bad day (or night) define this experience for you. The more you keep trying to be consistent with the routine, the more likely the good days will become your new norm.

The first full day was hard. I got her out of her crib at seven a.m. on the dot and fed her a bottle. After, we played and sang songs while I simultaneously tried to drink a coffee, unload the dishwasher, and inhale a granola bar. Fifteen minutes before her first nap, we started her wind-down routine. I changed her diaper and zipped her into a sleep sack before dimming the lights and turning on the white noise machine (I was establishing all those as cues to her that she was getting ready to sleep). Brown instructed me to rock her in the glider and sing her songs until she appeared to become sleepy, at which time I would place her in the crib. The important thing was to not put her down already asleep. Ideally, I was trying to find that sweet spot of "just sleepy enough" that she'd fall asleep on her own without much of a fight. She needed to build the confidence to know she could do it without my help, not to mention that it had to feel a bit scary to fall asleep in one place and wake up in another (gotta love those college years!).

As soon as her head hit the crib sheet, she started fussing. I let her try to work it out on her own for a few minutes before going back into the nursery. I used my voice to settle her down while patting her on her little belly. Once she quieted, I tried to sneak out of the room, only to hear her start fussing the moment the door shut behind me. I stood next to the door for a few more minutes, texting Brown incessantly, barraging her with rolling updates that she definitely hadn't asked for, before going back in to calm Tallulah.

For the better part of sixty minutes, this was our dance. At first it seemed futile, but Brown assured me that it was a process, like learning to ride a bike. I couldn't do it for her. Tallulah was absolutely capable of doing it on her own, and she would! After an hour, we scrapped the first nap and decided to try again for naps two and three, but they were equally disastrous. She cried and I cried, as I bounced in and out of the room. I questioned my decision and texted Brown again, telling her that maybe my daughter was the exception and not the rule. Perhaps her method wouldn't work for our family? She was calm and supportive and reminded me that nothing about this made me a bad mom. And by four o'clock in the afternoon, she even gave me license to pour myself a glass of wine, turn off the monitor, and sit in the backyard for five minutes to allow my nerves to settle. Then, try again.

That evening Tallulah passed out on my chest from sheer exhaustion, and I was so disheartened with the whole process that I considered abandoning the plan and told Brown as much, but she reminded me that I was doing what I thought was best for my daughter and that she had warned me it would get harder before it got easier (which is really just a testament of parenthood on the whole). She encouraged me to try again tomorrow, after which we could reassess if there was still no progress. It felt like a fair deal.

Early into our second day, I saw a glimmer of hope. Before Tallulah's first nap, we began the wind-down routine and I could see that she started to relax. She was responding to the cues, and her body knew that rest was coming. Tallulah fell asleep for about thirty minutes during her first nap (after only about twenty minutes of fussing). For her second nap, she only cried for about ten minutes. She didn't fall asleep, but she eventually calmed down and lay there quietly to rest. I didn't even need to go into the room! She was beginning to feel comfortable and safe in her little space, and that was the goal! To be fair, the third nap was a total train wreck, and I didn't even ask for Brown's permission before pouring myself a glass of wine and retreating, briefly, to the backyard.

On the third day, like some Houdini shit, Tallulah actually started to get the hang of things. Our routine wasn't perfect by any means, but she started to fuss less, quiet down sooner, and eventually fall asleep for extended periods all on her own.

Some people might think that what I put my daughter through constitutes torture, but I couldn't disagree more. If anything, I would suggest that my constant and horribly off-key singing, the kind where I hit notes only dogs could hear, has been far more damaging to her than letting her cry through a half-dozen naps back in February 2015.

CREEPY LULLABIES THAT YOU SHOULD AVOID SINGING TO YOUR CHILDREN

Three blind mice, three blind mice,
see how they run, see how they run.
They all ran after the farmer's wife,
Who cut off their tails with a carving knife.

[I am terrified of mice, but even this is a little too dark.]

London Bridge is falling down,
Falling down, falling down.

[I have a crippling fear of heights: skyscrapers, Ferris wheels, bridges, steep overpasses . . . this song is far from comforting.]

Rock-a-bye baby, in the treetop,
When the wind blows, the cradle will rock.
When the bough breaks, the cradle will fall,
And down will come baby, cradle and all.

[Um, postpartum anxiety much? The fear of my baby falling, or suffering any ailment, literally keeps me up at night. I don't need a nursery rhyme to add fuel to the fire.]

Ring-a-round the rosie,
A pocket full of posies,
Ashes! Ashes!
We all fall down.

[I mean, who isn't a fan of subtle bubonic plague references? Try explaining to a toddler that "Ashes! Ashes! We all fall down" is a reference to death and cremation. Awesome!]

Rub-a-dub-dub, three men in a tub.
And who do you think they were?
The butcher, the baker,
The candlestick maker

["Oh, hey, I'm just here for the gang bang!" Do you really need me to explain this one?]

* * *

Over the next few weeks, we found sweet relief. With adequate sleep, Tallulah emerged as a happier, more content baby. We established a routine that not only worked for the baby but also gave me a few hours of freedom here and there to regain my sanity, which is one of the many advantages of establishing a routine. Even if your day has totally fallen apart and feels entirely overwhelming, just knowing that you'll have a ninety-minute break from parenting can save you from going bananas. In many ways, having a routine and schedule gives you more flexibility in your life than not.

I've said it before and I'll say it again: many roads lead to Rome, and just because something worked for me doesn't mean it's going to work for every family and every baby. If Tallulah and I didn't figure out a way for us both to get rest, we were destined to live together forever in our own version of Grey Gardens; but instead of being surrounded by old newspapers and cats, we'd live among a sea of out-of-date sleep-training books and partially deflated exercise balls.

I'm not here to debate the finer points of sleep-training philosophies (different strokes for different folks); I just want to share with you our journey. Tallulah started sleeping well, and to this day, she has really great sleep habits. It's true that she still can't fall asleep with any stimuli happening in or around her room, but that's a small price to pay for a well-rested child.

However, I am going to keep reminding you over and over again how important it is that both you and your baby get enough sleep. Not only does it afford you some highly coveted "me time" during the day, it also means that you'll finally take back your nights. If, as a new mama, you're only working with a partly charged battery, everything else is going to feel like an uphill battle. I'm not suggesting you find a way to clock in ten hours every night, but if you're not managing a decent amount of consistent sleep, you might need to rework your game plan because it won't be long before you snap.

Without knowing it, Brown became one of the first members of my mama village. She listened to me bitch and moan, and because she was removed from my inner circle, I felt safe telling her just how difficult it all was. She nodded and would say things like, "It's so hard, I know." She offered me the gift of empathy and compassion, and gave me the freedom to be frustrated and defeated. She encouraged me to find small escapes from the madness, even if that meant taking five minutes in the backyard without judgment or opinion. She wasn't just helping me train my daughter how to sleep; she was training me how to be a mom as well.

Motherhood really is a sacrifice, and I was beginning to learn that lesson; most importantly, I was becoming okay with it. More than that, I was actually beginning to like it. Tallulah was getting older, turning into the playful, funny, smart little girl she was destined to become. Now that we were both getting a decent amount of rest, I was no longer drifting through my day on eggshells. I could start planning for our life together. We started going to baby music classes on the weekends and had stroller dates with friends. We'd blow bubbles in the backyard and take Archie to the dog park (where she'd go crazy laughing at all the dogs going wild). I guess, in some way, she started to become that "take your baby everywhere" kid; the path there was just a bit different from what I expected.

It's no great secret that around the time you start enjoying motherhood is around the time you start enjoying your kid, which usually coincides with when he or she starts sleeping with some regularity. The craziness begins to fade, and new parents emerge from the fog of newborn war. From there on, the road doesn't necessarily get easier, but it becomes more manageable, and the journey begins to feel so incredibly worth it. It's true what they say: in twenty years, you probably won't even remember all the shit you had to go through. But to get to that point, you still have to survive it.

12 "LEAN IN" TO HIGH-WAISTED DENIM: LEARNING TO LOVE YOUR MOM BOD

She was twenty-four years old, twenty-five, tops. Her black metallic sports bra had fashionable straps and buckles that crisscrossed in the front and back—like some sort of dominatrix athlete—holding in her tasteful Beverly Hills boob job. She pulled her thick black hair off her flawless olive complexion and into a pristine ponytail, while her lululemons slung low on her hips to reveal not a single ounce of fat.

Suddenly very aware of my own disheveled appearance, I adjusted my oversized, faded yellow tank, pulling the cheap cotton fabric off my stomach to keep it from sticking to my muffin top. My own sports bra had seen better days; the once-white straps poking out from under my shirt now had a grayish tinge. My hair, which hadn't been washed in a week, was thrown on top of my head in a greasy bun à la Britney circa 2008 (which we all know was not a good year for the pop princess). I had stopped breastfeeding about three months earlier and my body was apparently still adjusting to yet another shift in hormones, the symptoms of which included a bout of acne befitting a tween in puberty and tufts of hair cracking off at the roots.

COPING WITH YOUR POSTPARTUM HAIR

The postpartum hair struggle can be really debilitating, especially for women with fine hair. I fondly refer to my own as the "crown of thorns" (the breakage around the hairline that forced me to curate an impressive collection of hats). It's a common issue for so many new moms, but it's one that can feel particularly frustrating. Lucky for you, I got us a little bit of advice from the queen of fabulous hair, Alli Webb, founder of Drybar:

- Shampoo your hair only twice a week to allow the natural oils from your scalp to nourish your hair.
- If your hair is in a fragile state, go easy on heat styling (read: blow-dryers and hot tools). When you do, use heat protection products to help keep your hair hydrated.
- Biweekly hair masks can go a long way toward strengthening weak, compromised hair.
- Sleep on a satin pillow case. Cotton can be really rough on your hair, causing friction and damage.
- If your hair isn't feeling healthy, avoid highlighting or bleaching.
- Certain supplements definitely help. I recommend seeing a medical professional (either an internal medicine doctor or a hormone specialist) to find out which specific deficiencies you might have that may be causing hair issues.

Yet somehow I managed to snag the one spot in Barry's Bootcamp next to fucking Pacific Island Barbie. Not only had she obviously never had a baby, I'd also venture to guess that she'd never seen a single carb or gram of refined sugar. While my ass was shoved into my workout pants, with the seams screaming for dear life, she wore her ensemble as if it had been painted on her perfectly round behind. She was toned, but not overly muscular. She was thin, but not too skinny. She was literally everything I wasn't, as the floor-to-ceiling mirror in front of us made painfully obvious.

During plank pose, I could not stop staring at her boobs. They had clearly never met the deathly suck of a frantic newborn or been engorged beyond measure because of a clogged duct. There was actual breast tissue north of the nipple instead of just the deflated remains where the stream of life once ran. At the end of class, she offered me a smile and a "good workout!," which made me feel cheap and pathetic. She felt sorry for me, and that made my jealousy turn to absolute bitterness.

My daughter was nearly six months old, but it felt like eons since I had been pregnant, and I couldn't manage to escape my postpartum physique. Of course, I had tremendous respect for what my body did (in creating human life), but I still didn't want to live in my pregnant skin forever. And, as anyone can tell you, twenty-four weeks with a newborn can feel like a lifetime.

In the weeks and months postpartum, I had become a human Mrs. Potato Head experiment gone horribly wrong. My midsection looked like my stomach had been slowly pulled away from my body like a slingshot, before quickly snapping back (which is pretty much what happened), causing everything to appear disarranged and lumpy, and my C-section scar ran from hipbone to hipbone (and turned up at one end like a strange smiling Elvis). After breastfeeding and engorgement puffed my chest up about three sizes, the deflated aftermath was a mess: a fried egg hanging on a nail, as one friend put it, with nipples that clearly belonged to an orangutan.

Worst of all, I had plateaued in my postpartum weight loss and couldn't shake the last fifteen pounds (word of warning, after baby number two, it's even more determined to stick around). For someone who struggled with eating issues for much of her life, this was a real challenge. I managed to be active most days (which was a luxury, I know). I was dieting, juicing, and largely avoiding french fries, but the weight was not budging. It felt like I would be permanently stranded in that "flowy top" phase and in the jeans I wore religiously after a two-week food and beverage tour of Europe in 2011. I was doing everything I could to regain some sense of self but failing miserably on all fronts.

I knew it was normal and that my recovery would take time; after all, my body was undergoing the largest and most impactful transition of a woman's life. "Nine months on, nine months off" is the adage most people adhere to, but eighteen months felt like a really long time to be uncomfortable in my own skin. And it didn't help that everywhere I looked, I couldn't seem to escape the beautiful unicorn moms who seemed to defy all postpartum conventions. For these fantastical creatures, the weight just melted off and their bodies returned to their perfect pre-baby shape.

For the last decade or so, Kardashian Kulture, as I fondly refer to it, has taken a firm grip on this cultural narrative and we're bombarded with images of celebrities and personalities who are all too eager to show us their "bikini body after baby." When interviewed, they always chalk up their seemingly impossible rebound to Mother Nature's weight loss miracle, "breastfeeding," or even more annoyingly, the "good genes" excuse. They never make mention of the trainers, private chefs, aestheticians, and glam squads at their disposal. Or Photoshop. And normal women, like you and me and Chrissy Teigen, are trained to believe that our bodies and minds will snap back into selfie shape in no time at all.

But my body was not snapping back, which was causing *me* to snap.

"I need boobs," I announced, barreling into the house after the fitness class.

"Huh?" my husband asked, clearly taken aback by the Tasmanian she-devil whirling around and demanding plastic surgery.

"I can't live like this anymore," I said, tears forming and beginning to sting my hot, prickly skin. "I just feel disgusting." I collapsed onto the couch and gave myself the pity party I rightly deserved after being forced to compare myself to a beauty pageant contestant for the last sixty minutes.

"So . . . a boob job is gonna help with that?" he asked, tentatively.

Surely, the answer was no, but from where I stood, my boobs were the one thing I could fix immediately, and I was desperate for some kind of win. A friend of a friend had just had hers done by a doctor in Santa Monica who was known for his "natural, modest" approach to breast augmentation. Although I always assumed I would wait until I was done having children to do any sort of "enhancements," I started wondering if I would ever be comfortable enough with my body in its current state to actually go about the business of creating another baby.

"Babe," my husband began, "you know I think you look beautiful, right?"

"Yeah." I continued to sulk

"But I'll support whatever decision you feel is best for your body."

My jaw nearly hit the floor. Was this fucking fool kidding me? Yes, I ultimately wanted him to support me, but I was expecting him to be *aghast* over my request to go under the knife and at least put up a bit of a fight. I was waiting for him to say, "Leslie, you don't need to do that. You're perfect just as you are . . ." blah, blah, blah. Two years earlier, I had told him that I wanted to get Botox because I hated a line in my forehead and he exploded: "I don't want you putting that shit in your face!" But now, when I wanted to go under general anesthesia to have a doctor shove implants in my chest for the sake of having bigger boobs, he was all for female empowerment.

"Be less obvious!" I shouted, before getting up and storming out of the room.

To be fair, there was very little room for him to escape that conversation unscathed, but agreeing to foot the bill for the procedure was reason enough for me to eventually forgive him.

Okay, so here's where I am supposed to tell you that we live in a culture that demands perfectionism of women, especially during our postpartum journeys. It's my responsibility to tell you to turn off the voices inside your head that say, "Heidi Klum did it in three weeks and so can you!" I'm supposed to tell you to allow your body the time and grace to recover from this tremendous life event—and you should and you must.

However, at a certain point we all need to get to a place where we feel good, which requires us to balance what our bodies need from us and what we need from our bodies. Finding that happy place is critical for our postpartum relationship with self. Women are capable of understanding the need and value in both schools of thought.

But here's the thing: if you're anything like me, this isn't really just about your body.

In the weeks and months after my daughter was born, I lost so much of who I was pre-baby. I was still coming to grips with this new reality, and I believed that my physical appearance and how I felt about myself when I looked in the mirror were some of the few things that I could actually exercise a microcosm of control over in my new postpartum world. Though it's my duty to warn new moms against buying into the Kardashian Kulture of postpartum womanhood, it doesn't make it any less frustrating to feel so disconnected from your former self. Everyone was reminding me to give myself time, but I was tired of waiting. I just wanted to go back to the old me.

And that's the real dick thing that I keep coming back to: you're never going to go back. At least, not all the way back.

We all eventually learn that life on the other side, with our kids, is so much better, richer, and more fulfilling, but that realization takes time, like all great things. So, in the interim, as we fumble to connect who we are with who we used to be, we tell ourselves that our bodies, for example, can be exactly the same postbaby as they were pre-baby—for 99.9 percent of all women, this just isn't true. Buying further into that just creates more pressure for us to achieve the impossible and prompts us to panic when shit doesn't go to plan.

Logically, it makes zero sense to expect our bodies to rebound to their former state. We are literally playing host to another human being for forty weeks or so, during which time he or she grows from a microscopic creature into a fully formed baby, weighing anywhere from five to ten pounds. Our uterus is something of a cocoon and grows to nearly five times its normal size, thereby pushing aside other vital organs and expanding our bone structure. During birth, an actual human being evacuates our bodies—and don't even get me started on what that process does to us.

My ribs widened during pregnancy and never went back to their original shape. I'm always gonna be just a little larger around the middle; that's just a fact. Luckily, I didn't have a collection of custom corsets, but I did have to part with quite a few dresses with some inflexible boning. Many expectant mamas, especially women who spend a lot of time on their feet, find that their feet grow up to a half size during pregnancy. It has something to do with weight distribution and pressure that cause our feet to spread out like mounds of smooshed Play-Doh. One of my friends who had an enviable collection of designer shoes was forced to part with them. Tragic.

Many mamas learn that, try as they might, nothing allows them to recapture the waistline of yesteryear. Some women (I was one of them after my second pregnancy) even experience a condition known as diastasis recti, an abdominal muscle separation that results from the uterus expanding, which, depending on the severity, can require intense physical therapy or even surgery to repair. And, as you've figured out by now, if you have chosen to breastfeed, your boobs are forever fucked. Sure, your large, brown, flying saucer nipples eventually return to a normal size and nice pinkish hue, but the longer you breastfeed, the more gnarly the result.

As postpartum women, we're scratching and clawing for any sense of normalcy or any return to our former existence because EVERYTHING seems so out of control. If our hormones quickly regulated, giving the gift of rational thought, or if we had the type of support that enabled us to return to our normal daily lives and reclaim our identity roles, maybe the body thing wouldn't be such a huge issue. But for many of us, it's the ONE thing we feel like we can actually do something about. Our minds may be a hot mess, and our schedules that once were filled with business meetings, lunch dates, and weekend getaways are now completely beholden to our baby, but if we can feel that we at least LOOK like our old selves, then maybe, just maybe, we have a shot at making it out of this newborn haze alive.

I'm not suggesting that everyone goes out and gets their boobs done. I'm just saying that for me, it was the right decision. I know it wasn't normal, but I'm okay with being not normal. Tallulah was seven months old when I decided to move forward with breast augmentation surgery (that's the fancy term for "boob job").

"You're definitely a strong candidate for this procedure," the doctor announced, putting away his measuring tape. His offices were in a posh medical building a few blocks off the beach, and his waiting room had a small beverage fridge lined with Pellegrinos and naturally flavored waters. There was an espresso machine and oversized photography books with pictures of rich people's dogs; this definitely wasn't a "covered by insurance" kind of place.

"My husband and I want to have more kids, eventually," I said. "Do you think I should wait until after we're done having kids?"

"Hmm," he started, "well, do you want your breasts to look different between now and then?"

It was a fair question. I nodded.

"Let's get you fitted with some sizes." He handed the nurse a piece of paper. "She'll set you up with different options in the size range you'd feel most comfortable in, but first let's get some photos."

We walked into a room with what I can only describe as a wall of breasts. Displayed before me were breast implant options of varying sizes, shapes, materials, and textures. It was a literal buffet of boobies!

"I just want to fill out my bras again," I said, but the nurse ignored me and busied herself with collecting a tray of samples. She asked me to stand, topless, in front of a machine as it photographed my existing chest from every angle, and each picture appeared on a large screen after being captured.

If I wasn't already sure I wanted to go through with the procedure, the brightly lit, high-resolution images projected before me would have surely done the trick. Actually, it was the clearest look I'd ever gotten of my own chest, and it wasn't pretty. By the time I left the office, I was armed with a folder of photos, paperwork, and images of what my chest would possibly look like at varying sizes postsurgery. When my husband got home from work that evening, I told him that I was going to stay on the conservative side of the doctor's recommendation.

"Do what you want, babe," he started, "but from what I hear most women wish they would have gone larger. . . ."

The art of subtlety has clearly never been his strongest quality.

Okay, so this is the part of the story where I'm supposed to have this huge epiphany. I'm supposed to realize that, as a nursing mother, my breasts sustained my child's life. I should be embracing my new mom bod and wearing my scars, my cellulite, and my new, slightly awkward breasts as badges of honor. I shouldn't be ashamed of how I look; I needed to recognize the miracles of the human body.

That's what I was supposed to do, but that's not what I did. I got a damn boob job. Look, I am well aware that putting this out there in the world is going to get me some major blowback. Someone somewhere is going to type up some nasty comments about how I'm speaking out of both sides of my ugly mouth. How I'm telling moms to ignore the social pressures and Instamom phenomenon and totally subscribing to it. What crazy lady runs and gets a boob job after having a baby? (***Raises hand slowly***)

Honestly, I totally understand their point. It's not normal! It also isn't cheap, so it's not an option for all the women who consider it (it took me two years to pay off those bad boys). I know certain people may judge me for focusing so much on my appearance postpartum, but it was something that I needed to do for me. I felt deformed. Whether or not another woman would feel the same way in my skin, I don't know, but that's just how I felt. I wanted to look in the mirror and not feel like I was going to cry. My breasts had changed as a result of pregnancy and nursing; they would never be the same and I did what I needed to do in order to accept that.

Two weeks after the consultation, I went in for surgery. People often wonder whether I was nervous about going under anesthesia with such a young child at home or scared about being cut open, but my answer is always no. I literally had an eight-pound human pulled out of my stomach; this was a piece of cake.

Once again, let me be clear: this is NOT an advertisement for postpartum women to get breast implants after they have a baby (although it may sound a little bit like it at times). Actually, what I did is nutty, but a mother's journey to reclaim her sense of self is complex and hard fought. This was a decision I made because my breast tissue was so severely damaged by the complications I experienced while breastfeeding, and my postpartum body was doing a number on my head.

Three months after the surgery, I began seeing a chiropractor. Unbeknownst to me, the constant pressure of carrying my daughter around on my left hip had exacerbated a back injury I got during high school (I took a long fall off a very tall horse, which resulted in a metal stirrup being jammed into my back with remarkable force). The doctor suggested I see the acupuncturist to help remove some of the immediate pressure. She asked how I was settling into my postpartum body, and I opened up about my battle to get back to me, and explained that it wasn't until I was on hiatus recovering from breast augmentation that I actually began losing the last of the weight.

"Go figure!" I joked.

"Well," she started, "it sounds like your body finally felt safe enough to let go of the weight."

"What do you mean?"

"Your body was probably in fight-or-flight mode," she explained. Apparently, during that postpartum tailspin, my body thought I was being hunted down by a saber-toothed tiger or a woolly mammoth or some shit; it was clinging to the last of my weight (read: fat) because it thought I was on the run and would need the fuel. I was in a futile race against myself to try to be someone I'd never be again.

The surgery forced me to hit pause for a few weeks while I recovered, and, miraculously, my body started to recalibrate on its own. The pounds disappeared. As my hormones balanced, my skin bounced back and my hair grew again. Giving myself that small, B-cup-sized victory allowed me the chance to breathe, and during that brief respite, my body naturally did what thousands of years of evolution trained it to do.

And—you're not going to love this—it wasn't until Tallulah's first birthday that I started to feel like myself again because that's when I became more comfortable with the "new me." It took that long for all the components of my new mom life—the emotional, the physical, and the mental—to establish some sort of balance. That isn't to say "don't bother even trying until your kid is one"; you need to do what is best for your psyche when it comes to your physicality postbaby, which is the real point I'm getting at. Once I started to regain my confidence, I was a happier woman, and being a happier woman allowed me to be a better, more patient and caring mom. All this shit is interrelated. It's so exhausting.

I am actually very grateful for everything my body did for me and my children. It may not seem that way, but it's true. I am allowed to respect my body for what it is capable of and do things for myself to feel comfortable in my own skin. I needed to find my path forward to embracing this new body, to finding comfort and acceptance. When I stopped trying to force myself into my old shell, I finally found peace in the new woman I had become. My hips are always going to be a bit wider; I'm always going to have a scar. There are some stretch marks here and there, and some pounds that will never go away. I have a few more grays, a few more fine lines, and constant dark circles. I'm finally okay with it. I look at my daughter and can hardly believe that I made her. Every inch of her is sheer perfection, and I created her in my body. And that is a fucking miracle.

13

SHAME OVER: TURNING OFF THE OUTSIDE NOISE

"I can only speak for myself, but I didn't have children just so they could be raised by a nanny."

She said it casually enough for the statement to seem relatively innocuous, and though it wasn't aimed directly at me, she said it loud enough that I—a working mom who recently acquired full-time childcare—could hear.

My husband and I had joined a handful of friends for Sunday brunch, and I was in the middle of a conversation of my own when I heard this comment tossed out from across the dining table. At the time, my daughter was eight months old and I had already been on the receiving end of some pretty ridiculous comments—like when I accompanied a pregnant friend to an appointment with her obstetrician weeks after giving birth to Tallulah and her doctor offered me a sincere apology when I told her I had had a C-section (I was more surprised than upset, because I legitimately didn't know how defective people thought I was until that moment). As a new mom, you never know what's going to roll off your back and what's going to stick to your soul like glue. You may not know your biggest parenting insecurity until you're forced to come face-to-face with it, and this "nanny" remark just got all up in my grill.

A few months earlier, I had begun working on a new project that was keeping me out of the house for longer hours than I would have liked and, as a result, I started suffering from some pretty major mom guilt (which I'll dive into more in Chapter 15). Of all the comments this woman could have made, this remark at this particular time shot an arrow right through my maternal Achilles' heel because it was something I was already struggling with. Whether or not it was intended for my ears (I'm sure it was), it was a pretty tone-deaf thing to say considering my situation—and my obvious proximity to the conversation.

Not to mention, she didn't know my circumstances. Maybe I couldn't afford to stay at home. I'm sure there are plenty of mothers who would prefer to stay home with their children, but it isn't financially possible. Lots of new moms don't have the luxury of not having to produce an income. They *must* work to support their family. Even though I knew better, this not-so-thinly-veiled criticism really shook me up.

Prior to having a baby, I made no secret of the fact that I planned to continue working. Not only was it in the best interest of my family, but it was also in the best interest of me. I needed to continue writing and creating for my own sanity; it was a part of my identity. This person, on the other hand, had always expressed a desire to stay at home once she and her husband started a family.

Up until this point, I thought we had a mutual respect for each other's choices when it came to this particular topic, understanding that no one road leads to Rome and we were each choosing the path best for us. So I was hurt and confused as to why she would wait this long to vocally express her negative opinion of me and my decision—especially in front of so many people.

I wondered whether my friend really thought I was a shitty mom for leaving my little girl with a nanny. I wondered who else might feel this way. And, most importantly, I wondered . . . were they right? Of course I felt guilty about the times I wasn't with my daughter; but I couldn't very well be in two places at once. I was doing my best to juggle work life with home life, and I already felt incredibly anxious about how I was managing it all. This insult wasn't just a reflection of me; it was a reflection of me as a mother.

It would seem that in her eyes, I didn't have my child's best interests at heart and was somehow letting my baby girl down, when it was the opposite. I believed I was making the best possible choice for our family. Her snide remark implied that my decision to go back to work was the wrong one, and that Tallulah would suffer for it.

Tell me I'm a shitty writer; tell me I have terrible taste in home décor; tell me that my ass looks huge in those jeans . . . but do not tell me I'm letting down my child. I could deal with disappointing myself; I couldn't deal with disappointing my daughter.

I felt the primal need to defend myself but didn't have the balls to address the situation head-on. Instead, later that day, my husband became my de facto punching bag. I explained to him all the reasons why going back to work was the right decision for me, and how I would never think of judging another parent for his or her decision on how to best provide for their family.

"Leslie, none of that even matters," he said. "We decided to get a nanny because that was the best decision for us. End of story. You don't need to defend it to anyone."

I knew he was right, and appreciated the sentiment, but that's a hell of a lot easier said than done. When people criticize our capabilities as parents, it strikes at our most sensitive nerve—a nerve most of us didn't even know we had until our children were born. When women mom-shame, it comes from a place of insecurity about their own choices. No one wants to think they're the ones doing it wrong.

You can be shamed for going to work, and you can be shamed for staying home. No one is immune.

More often than not, becoming parents causes us to shift our priorities in a way that our children become our number one concern—and when others make us doubt our decisions or choices, it makes us feel like we're failing our most important responsibility. And what do you think that does to a woman who has given up so much of herself to be a mother? How does she feel if she believes that she sacrificed so much just to fail at parenthood?

Like so much of this book, falling prey to "mom shaming" is just another opportunity for us to doubt how amazing we are as mothers. Being part of the mom-shaming epidemic, whether dishing it out or taking it, is almost a rite of passage for women now as they transition into new motherhood. Family, friends, strangers, and even anonymous social media naysayers feel they have carte blanche to criticize our decisions. It's become so commonplace and has poured into our daily lives, somehow giving license to anyone with a pulse to judge someone else's motherhood experience.

The usual suspects in mom-shaming controversies range from opinions on placenta encapsulation to allowance of screen time and, the biggest culprit, how we choose to feed our babies (please refer to Chapter 9). However, it's not always the most blatant insults that can send a mom into a shame spiral. Currently, beneath the mom culture surface, there lurks a brand of mom shaming that is far more vicious and nuanced and quite different from the outwardly obvious comments made by a stranger in a grocery store or a coward hiding behind the protective veil of private or anonymous social media accounts. I have witnessed it on countless playgrounds and in the "safety" of certain baby groups. The biggest offenders for new moms are those subtle jabs, passive-aggressive critiques, sideways glances, and seemingly innocent commentary from other moms that can cause women to question their motherhood journey:

"You really shouldn't give her that much sugar."

"I'd never let my kids run around a restaurant like that."

"Isn't he too big for a stroller?"

"You should really have socks on that baby."

"Can't you just work while she naps?"

"Oh . . . he's still using a pacifier!"

"You can't stay for circle time? What could be more important than your son?"

"No thanks, my kids don't eat processed foods."

"My daughter was fully potty-trained by twenty months."

"I don't want to be *that* mom, but you shouldn't be using aerosol sunblock."

"Oh, wow! He stays up late!"

"Can you do something? I can hear your little girl talking." (Said to a mom at a performance of *The Nutcracker* . . . for kids.)

And, "I can only speak for myself, but I didn't have children just so they could be raised by a nanny."

Unless you've been parenting under a rock, it's safe to assume that you too have experienced some degree of mom shaming. And some of us may even be guilty of, once or twice, being on the wrong side of mom shaming. (***Raises hand reluctantly***)

For me, it was 2013, and I watched, horrified, as a mother of two attempted to situate her kids at a table at a popular lunch spot in Los Angeles. Disheveled and a bit frantic, this mama bulldozed into the place pushing an enormous tandem stroller before wrestling her twin toddlers into side-by-side high chairs, each one taking his turn to whine as the other received his mother's attention. When both children were secure in their seats, the mother collapsed into hers, produced a foam-covered iPad from the diaper bag, and plopped it in front of the kids. Each child took a hold of the foam arm closest to him (to ensure the other wouldn't steal the entire device).

I watched, gobsmacked, as this scene unfolded. Eventually, I turned my attention back to my lunch date, rolled my eyes, and said:

She's not going to come home from high school with a D in geometry because she watched the episode where "the pups save a baby octopus." (If anything, my own ineptitude with math would more likely be to blame.)

So, what right did I have to judge that woman with twins? I didn't. Just as my friend had no right to judge my struggle to balance being a working mother with what was best for my child. I'm not sure if that woman with twins heard my snide remark (if she did, I'm SO, SO sorry), but that's the thing about mom shaming. It may not be outwardly obvious; sometimes it isn't even visible to the childless eye.

As a family, we decided to hire a nanny to help us; it didn't matter the reason. It didn't matter if it was because we needed a second income or not; it didn't matter whether or not I had a prestigious career I couldn't abandon; it didn't even matter if I was a stay-at-home mom who just opted to have an extra pair of hands around because . . . BEING A MOM IS TOUGH!

Regardless of the reason, we made the best decision for our family, and as a grown-ass woman, I do not need to explain that to anyone else—not to friends, not to family, not to anyone.

But here's where I'm gonna take a turn. Instead of allowing myself to become enraged by this shit, I try really, really hard to have compassion for the people who make these remarks, particularly other mothers.

The motherhood bar today is set at such an unrealistic height, it's inevitable that we'll all eventually fail. It's much easier to bash someone else's journey than it is to admit that the way we're doing things isn't necessarily the best or only way.

There's no one correct way, and shaming other parents says less about them and more about us. We all love our kids and we want to be so resolute in our decisions that mom shaming—even if done unintentionally—comes far too easily. Not to mention, shaming someone else is almost always a megaphone shouting our own shortcomings, not necessarily a reflection of the other person. We prop ourselves up by putting other parents down. We want to affirm our own beliefs and decisions when it comes to raising kids, and unfortunately that can be at the expense of others. I really believed that my going to work was the best thing I could do for Tallulah. I knew that my husband and I could better provide for her by bringing in a second income, and I also knew that giving myself the opportunity to focus on my career would make me a more well-rounded mother, and a healthier woman.

We just all need to take a deep breath and remind ourselves that there are a hundred different ways to raise amazing kids, and just because someone is doing it differently from how we do it doesn't mean they're doing it wrong. Most importantly, don't let someone else have that power over you. Are they in your home? Did they carry your child and bring him or her into the world? No, you did. You're a motherfucking badass mom. You need to trust in your mama instincts and appreciate that not everyone is going to agree with every decision you make.

IN DEFENSE OF MOM SHAMING

Not to be a total hypocrite, but on the very rare occasion, I do support a mild amount of mom shaming. But only when it is *absolutely* deserved. Here are a few examples of when it's okay to throw a little mom shade:

» If you post poo pictures on social media. Don't post poo pictures. The internet is forever.

» If your maternity photo shoot includes any of the following: weaponry, taxidermy, political propaganda, or predatory animals.

» If you dress your child in Ed Hardy shirts or Von Dutch hats. Just stop.

- If on social media you ask for guidance on newborn sleeping or feeding, and then proceed to criticize the advice people are offering. If you don't want to hear it, don't ask!
- If you assume everyone wants to hold your baby for an hour. If I'm not forced to tote around my own kids, I like giving my arms a break. Some moms love holding someone else's kid, but it's good to check in. I'm okay for about 120 seconds before I'm ready to abandon ship. (Side note: I had quite a few friends push back on this criticism. To hear them tell it, it's every mom for herself. If you offer to hold the baby without really wanting to, then that's your mistake.)
- If your kid has a 102-degree fever and is coughing like a sixty-year-old smoker, but you still bring him to a birthday party and claim it's "teething." Same goes for hand, foot, and mouth disease.
- If you give your baby an eyebrow wax and/or spray tan.
- If you drive around with your newborn on your lap.
- And, finally, if you judge another mom for doing what she believes is best for her family, even if you don't agree with it.

\+ + +

And if you find yourself on the receiving end of hurtful remarks, don't get mad or upset. Try (hard as it can be) to find some compassion, because you know you're doing and have done your absolute best, and, unlike some people, you don't need to shit on anyone else to prove it.

Yes, I have full-time childcare and my children are healthy, happy, and thriving. Tallulah and I have an incredible bond, and she also has an amazing relationship with her nanny. And because I have childcare, I have managed to raise her while also having the opportunity to create a platform to support and encourage other mothers . . . oh, and I also wrote this book (and three others). So, yeah, I don't have to explain shit to anyone.

(Mic drop.)

14

NO, YOU CANNOT DO IT ALL: REWIRING HOW YOU VALUE SUCCESS

Like most women my age, I spent much of my adult life wanting desperately to be a Rachel Green: charming, quirky, casual, approachably beautiful, and impossibly cool. But try as I might, I am hopelessly and forever a Monica Geller: neurotic, competitive, obsessively clean, largely inflexible, and overwhelmingly brunette.

For the longest time, I wanted to be the sort of girl who could glide through life and just trust that everything would fall into place. Unfortunately, I wasn't born with that gene. Instead, I'm the type who becomes so anxious and compulsive that I have definitely manifested my "worst-case scenario" into reality on more than one occasion. I'm pretty sure that the February 2007 snowstorm that plowed into New York and left thousands of stranded passengers at JFK airport was largely my fault, because I spent weeks stressing over whether my flight to Las Vegas that day would be delayed (and it was, by about six hours).

At my wedding, the word used most to describe me during speeches was *organized*. If that doesn't spell romance, I don't know what does. During "ditch day" my senior year of high school, I was the only student to show up to seventh period Econ just in case there was a pop quiz. As a child, I spent summers devouring every book on the "Summer Reading List" and spent more time arranging my school supplies than I did swinging from trees. To this day, I'm hard pressed to find anyone willing to play Monopoly with me, and I've given myself the title of "Best Driver in the State of California."

I've only ever had one speed: overdrive. For my entire pre-baby life, I was used to doing everything at 100 percent capacity. That isn't to suggest that everything I did was accomplished to perfection but rather to completion. I don't like unfinished business, and therefore I plan. I plan for everything. I make lists, I color-code them, and then I make color-coded keys to decipher the existing lists. I wish I was joking.

As mentioned, by the time our daughter was born, I had already researched every piece of baby gear within an inch of its life—including embarking on a weeks-long saga on the ideal crib mattress. I believed that if I could prepare for every possible newborn hiccup, stage, and hurdle that I would have an easier time adjusting to my new normal. But as all mothers know, there was no way to escape my motherhood fate, and it was my job to surrender to her needs . . . because that's what moms do.

I was no longer the person in charge; I needed to follow her lead, and that was a sacrifice that did not come easy for me.

Being a mom and caring for a child—in addition to everything else—put limitations on how much I could accomplish in a day. I had trouble finding time to conquer the mundane and ordinary—showering, washing clothes, making my bed—because my most pressing obligation was my daughter.

Like clockwork, the sun would rise and then slip away again before I did anything that I considered productive (because I was clueless enough to think that sustaining a human life all on my own wasn't enough). For weeks at a time, it would feel like Groundhog Day and it even got to the point when my husband would call me on his way home from work just so I would have enough time to change out of my pajamas before he got home.

For the first few months, I could rationalize my limitations because "I just had a baby" (on the rare occasion when I was able to be rational), but the older she got, the cheaper that excuse felt.

Tallulah was about five months old when I started working again, and though the chaotic days of newborn life were then behind me, I still struggled to keep everything afloat. Each day brimmed with expectation and my to-do list grew to a mile long as more and more fell through the cracks and got tacked on the end. Life began to feel like a bunch of full-time jobs that I was shoving into a part-time schedule. Mostly, I kept my chin up, because nervous breakdowns were a luxury of time I did not have. I'd routinely remind myself that "If you're going through hell, keep going," because Winston Churchill wartime quotes were an appropriate motherhood comparison.

A LIST OF POLITICAL QUOTES THAT SHOULDN'T APPLY TO MOTHERHOOD . . . BUT DO

"Speak softly and carry a big stick."

—THEODORE ROOSEVELT

"Do I not destroy my enemies when I make them my friends?"

—ABRAHAM LINCOLN

"I am extraordinarily patient, provided I get my own way in the end."

—MARGARET THATCHER

"If we give up now, we forsake a better future."

—Barack Obama

"Never retreat, never retract . . . never admit a mistake."

—Napoleon Bonaparte

"You have to be prepared to accept that you are not going to get 100 percent approval."

—Hillary Clinton

"In the truest sense, freedom cannot be bestowed; it must be achieved."

—Franklin D. Roosevelt

"I have thought it my duty to exhibit things as they are, not as they ought to be."

—Alexander Hamilton

"We're not perfect, and there are some dark patches in our past, but what makes us special is that we recognize these evils, we come to grips with them, and we fix them."

—Dianne Feinstein

"Service which is rendered without joy helps neither the servant nor the served."

—Mahatma Gandhi

"Organize, agitate, educate, must be our war cry."

—Susan B. Anthony

"If you succeed, there are many rewards; if you disgrace yourself, you can always write a book."

—Ronald Reagan

Even though Tallulah was sleeping through the night, I was lucky to clock six hours. I would find myself down a Pinterest rabbit hole looking up toddler foods or craft projects; I'd stay up researching behavior and development; but mostly, I would end up watching mind-numbing shows on Bravo because I just needed to zone out for a little while. My days began in a groggy blur and ended when I was physically incapable of keeping my eyes open any longer. It was exhausting and maddening, but the crazy thing was that as long as my day went somewhat to plan, I could manage to juggle everything I needed to juggle.

But life doesn't always work like that; in fact, it usually doesn't.

My husband and I lived in one of those adorable midcentury Hollywood bungalows built right into the side of Benedict Canyon, with lots of charming windows, original wood flooring, and less-than-stellar plumbing. It wasn't very kid-friendly (lots of steep stairs) and the entire foundation was on a bit of a tilt, but it was peaceful. Just two miles north of the hustle and bustle of Sunset Boulevard, our neighborhood was a woodsy canyon sanctuary crawling with critters. We would hear owls at night, see coyotes and deer scurry off into the hills, and catch gophers popping up from their hillside burrows. We had a family of wolf spiders colonize our balcony (which wasn't cute) and a snake moved into our garage.

Fortunately, due in large part to my borderline compulsive tendencies, the inside of our house stayed pest-free until right before Tallulah's first birthday. The hottest time of year in Los Angeles is often the early fall, and this particular October was no exception. And just like humans, bugs *love* air-conditioning.

One morning, I woke up early to get Tallulah and myself ready for a mommy and me class, and that's when I first discovered them. Initially, the black granite counters concealed the invasion. I went to make coffee and saw a few ants crawling across the silver dial of the Nespresso machine. I pressed my finger on them and washed my hands. I pulled a spoon out of the drawer and spotted about a dozen little ants scattering across the silverware. Disgusted, I picked up the entire divider tray and dumped it in the sink.

I opened the cabinet where I kept Tallulah's bottles, thinking it was safe because it was above the counter, but that's when I saw them: an army of ants creeping and crawling all over my baby's clean, sterilized bottles. In full-blown panic mode, I pulled all of the bottles and sippy cups out and tossed them in the sink. I looked in the pantry and found another herd of ants covering our Tupperware, snacks, pouches, chips, and everything else. The trail of insects stretched down out of the pantry, across the baseboards, and into every inch of our kitchen. It was a full-blown enemy attack. I called for my husband (who must have thought I found a body on the kitchen floor), and he came running.

"They're EVERYWHERE," I shouted. I started pulling everything out of the pantry and the cabinets. I crawled around on the floor following the trail of ants to a small hole under the kitchen island.

This is ruining the entire morning!

Instead of being able to spend the next ninety minutes getting Tallulah breakfast and preparing for the day, I had to spend it cleaning out my entire kitchen and spraying it down with the sort of totally organic, nonchemical bug spray that doesn't actually work. We'd go to our toddler class, and I would spend the entire time distracted and disengaged, and instead of being able to work when I got home, I'd have to keep cleaning the kitchen and call a pest control company, before going to the grocery store to rebuy everything I had just thrown in the trash (which would get me thinking about what a waste of money this ordeal was and how I needed to work to make money, but how the hell was I going to work today?).

I was trying so hard to keep everything together, but at any given moment I was one misstep away from completely crumbling. There was zero flexibility in my day, literally no room for error.

But errors are the baseline of the motherhood experiment. Whether it's an ant infestation, a sick baby who can't go to day care, or a washing machine malfunction, a new mom is juggling an insane amount and, eventually, balls will drop. I was kidding myself to think the day would go off without a hitch, especially on a day when I really needed it to. The ants weren't nearly the catastrophe I made them out to be (but still a huge bummer) but rather the straw that broke the back of this totally burned-out camel.

For so long, much of my own value and worth rested on my ability to balance and juggle all the different aspects of my life, and, after becoming a mother, I was utterly frustrated when it all crumbled to pieces. Every week, I bounced from work meetings and networking events to playdates and music classes, while trying to continue my writing career. I researched potty training, preschools, and dealing with tantrums while grocery shopping and doing the laundry, the cooking, and the cleaning.

I was scheduling doctor appointments, vet visits, dinners, and holiday plans. I was trying to be present with my baby girl, trying to connect with my friends and family, and trying to enjoy the time I had with my husband. I would spend countless hours on Amazon ordering whatever it was that kept arriving on my doorstep in Prime boxes each day—yet, somehow, I never got around to ordering hairspray or bodywash for myself. And . . . I was really fucking tired.

Since she arrived, I'd gone from playing a calculated, precise game of chess to scrambling around a game of fifty-two-card pickup. Instead of being thorough and thoughtful about projects, obligations, and the work in front of me, I spent my days putting out the next biggest fire.

When I went to go see my therapist, I unloaded on him. I told him all about our ant infestation and how tremendously it seemed to affect me; it caused a domino effect that I was incapable of handling. I had too much responsibility and not enough time.

"I'm used to doing everything in my life to a hundred percent," I explained. "I don't cut corners. I don't do the minimum, especially when I know that I can do better. But now, I'm *lucky* if I can accomplish anything with seventy percent of my effort or attention."

To me, that was as good as failing. At best, I was rocking a C average when it came to the most important things in my life: my daughter, my work, my husband, and myself. We all deserved better than a C. That was unacceptable! And if anyone deserved my 100 percent, it was my daughter.

"Well," my therapist began, "perhaps you just need to reset your expectations. What you feel is only seventy percent of what you were capable of before children might now be your hundred percent."

Which, to me, translated to: get comfortable with your mediocrity because the phrase is "Keepin' it 100." I have yet to hear someone say that they're "Keepin' it 70."

I wasn't raised to just get by. For better or worse, I always knew that being a woman meant I would have to work harder to get the same recognition as a man, which meant spending more time in the office. More time in the office meant I had to be more efficient in my daily life. Surrendering to the limitations of time meant that I would be sacrificing something, and that was never an option. Whether or not that was a healthy attitude is debatable, but either way, that's how I lived my pre-baby life.

Being able to do it all was how I determined my self-worth, so when I became a mom and had no time to do anything beyond care for my child, I constantly felt like I was fumbling. If I did manage to carve out a small part of the day for me or for my work or for my home, I felt like my baby suffered as a result. No matter how I chose to divide and conquer my day, I could never get in front of the ball.

Ultimately, I needed to continue learning how to relinquish control. I'm not gonna be able to do everything at 100 percent, and sometimes 70 percent is just going to have to be good enough. (Unless it's a glass of wine, in which case, no excuses! Play like a champion!)

New moms need to practice the art of giving themselves grace. And I, for one, need to listen to my own advice. Sure, I may have as many hours in the day as Beyoncé, but I don't have an army of support staff to keep this train moving forward (or even on the tracks). I also don't have a wind machine following me around making me feel like a walking, talking Vidal Sassoon commercial while I vacuum my living room.

TIPS FOR NOT GOING FUCKING CRAZY

- ***Be practical.*** The worst thing you can do is set yourself up for failure by stacking the odds against you. This means recognizing that life is going to be messy and giving yourself a buffer for when things go wrong. Don't schedule your day down to the minute or expect to be able to run three errands between nap times. Be realistic with your time and energy.
- ***Outsource.*** We live in an era when there is an app for just about everything. Sure, it often comes with a price tag, but what is your sanity worth? From laundry services and on-call handymen (or women!) to getting your groceries delivered and finding doctors who make house calls (and take insurance!), there are options out there that can help lighten your load.
- ***Get organized.*** If you collapse into bed each night only to wake up to another day of chaos, of course you're going to go crazy! An easier morning makes for a better overall day. Take fifteen minutes before bed and do what you can to help yourself out: make some overnight oats and pack lunches, organize the diaper bag, lay out clothes, and so on. The less you have to do in the morning the better!
- ***Cry if you want to.*** Don't feel like you always need to be this steeple of strength. Sometimes a good cry is exactly what you need . . . and some ice cream.
- ***Prioritize.*** Every day, make one thing a priority and allow everything else to be secondary. The next day, switch it up. Of course, this is more of a challenge for working moms, but you can easily apply this idea to weekends and days at home. One day, make getting your house in order a priority; the next day, make quality time with

your baby a priority; the next day, make errands outside the house a priority; the next day, make your partner or yourself a priority, and so on. The idea is that you can't give 100 percent of yourself to everything every day, but you can give 100 percent of yourself to everything on specific days.

» ***Fill your own tank.*** A happy mom is a healthy mom; a healthy mom is someone who takes time for herself. It doesn't have to be every day, but once a week afford yourself the time to enjoy something you're passionate about: reading, exercising, *Real Housewives*.

» ***Choose quality over quantity.*** This is especially true for working moms. It's easy to get stressed out about being a "bookends" parent, but the amount of time you spend with your child isn't nearly as important as the quality of that time. If you can carve out twenty minutes each day to put down the phone, get on the floor, and just *be* with your little person, I guarantee it is more meaningful than hours of them watching you be stressed out and staring at your email.

» ***Don't compare.*** Stop looking at other families and wondering how they seem to manage it better than you do, because I can pretty much guarantee they're wondering the same thing about you!

I'm not convinced that I simply needed to lower my expectations, as my therapist suggested. Instead, I needed to reevaluate what I consider a win. There will be days when I am able to dance backward in high heels, and there will be days when the most I can do is simply get out of bed and go through the motions. The important thing to remember here is that one single day does not define any woman.

For instance, when you have planned your day down to the minute and life decides to hurl an ant infestation into your lap, instead of collapsing under the mounting pressure of responsibilities, you just need to adjust. You need to remind yourself of the incredible work you do every day to keep your family afloat and that you routinely do the work of three men. So, if one day gets super fucked up and you need to trash all of your plans, that is okay because you spend every other day juggling fire. Allow yourself to relish the small accomplishments and give yourself a pass on the shit that goes sideways. And, yes, sometimes simply taking a shower is the best you can do, so celebrate the fuck outta that win!

When my son was born, I forced myself to indulge in the early days with him when no one expected me to do much. I knew that within a few weeks, I would be back to the grind of juggling fire and trying to keep my family (and myself) afloat, so I was better able to appreciate the moments when the only thing I truly needed to do was to be a mama.

Is it a constant battle of conflicting needs and shifting priorities? Absolutely. Do I collapse into bed most nights unsure how I'll get through the next week? Absolutely. Do I want to pursue a career but also try to be home with my kids as much as possible? Absolutely. But, at the end of the day, would I have my life any other way? Absolutely not. I guess the answer is, I'm not looking for shit to change; I just want the right to bitch about it.

15

YOU'RE NOT CAUSING PERMANENT DAMAGE: THE DAILY STRUGGLE WITH MOM GUILT

Am I fucking up my kids?

This is my greatest fear as a mother, and one that runs through my head every day. The mom guilt is real, y'all, and it can often feel debilitating because I'm constantly second-guessing myself. I'm worried that I'm going to do something so catastrophically wrong that I'm going to mess my children up indefinitely.

No matter what we do, or how much we do, there is always something to feel guilty about. Mom life is a double-edged sword; we just need to decide which side of the blade to fall on. The guilt and fear of messing up our kids is something most moms struggle with, but it still feels like such an isolating concern. Many of us aren't talking about these worries or sharing our anxieties with other parents because we're petrified of how it might make us look. Even more, we're terrified to discover that other moms don't feel the same way, which thereby reaffirms our fears that we are, in fact, royally screwing up.

Isn't it horrible? So many moms suffer in silence simply because they're afraid of the response they might get! Although I think mom guilt looms larger over time, I think that for many of us, the guilt begins the moment we realize we're pregnant:

Oh shit! I was pregnant when I went on that roller coaster.

Oh shit! I was pregnant and drank so much champagne.

Oh shit! I was pregnant when I got Botox.

I literally did all three of these before I knew I was pregnant with my son, and these pre–pregnancy test "whoops!" moments were just the tip of the iceberg. Most of this book focuses on my transition into motherhood when I had my daughter in 2014, because that incredible little girl barreled into my world like a pint-sized bull into my very curated china shop—and because, for most of us, often the most challenging moments of motherhood come the first time around when we don't know what the hell we're doing. That being said, the mom guilt I experienced throughout my pregnancy with my son was so crippling and anxiety-inducing that I couldn't possibly write this chapter without sharing it.

My husband and I had been trying to get pregnant with our second child for months and months. Tallulah was one of those "first try" wonders, and even though I told myself that I wasn't going to catch lightning in a bottle the second time around, somewhere deep down I was still expecting to.

Every month, I took the early pregnancy tests a few days before my period, praying for one to be positive, but nothing. It was a tedious cycle that we endured for the better part of a year before finally deciding to talk to my obstetrician. She suggested that we consider seeing a specialist, because a "natural" pregnancy (I hate that term; all pregnancies are natural, some of us just need assistance) might not be possible for us.

We found a specialist through the recommendation of a friend, and he said that before doing any treatments, I needed to first have a hysterosalpingogram (HSG)—an X-ray procedure in which a doctor shoots dye through your uterus and fallopian tubes to detect any abnormalities and to make sure there are no blockages. (Yes, it was as uncomfortable as it sounds.)

Unbeknownst to me, I was already three weeks pregnant. The pregnancy tests were negative, and then I had what I assume was a phantom period (a term I still don't fully understand). How could I have known? But that's the thing—something doesn't have to be rational or logical for you to feel guilty about it.

When I finally discovered I was pregnant, four weeks later, the main concern wasn't the roller coaster, the champagne, or even the Botox; it was putting my unborn child through the HSG procedure. Not only did I expose him to radiation, but also the dye posed the risk of detaching him from my uterine wall. It goes without saying that expecting mothers should *not* get HSGs (and, no, I was not asked to do a pregnancy test prior to the procedure). In the very few cases of women undergoing an HSG while pregnant, a majority ended in miscarriage shortly after.

All I wanted was this baby. All I hoped for was this baby. And something I did to my body could cause me to lose my baby. If that isn't a ripe occasion for some paralyzing fucking mom guilt, I don't know what is.

Unfortunately, the guilt didn't end there. Ten days after learning I was pregnant, without warning, I started bleeding. It wasn't the brown spotting that pregnancy blogs warn you about; this was a bright-red flood. I screamed for my husband, who was putting our daughter to sleep, and he found me in the bathroom.

"This is it," I sobbed, my head in my hands as he rubbed my back. "I'm losing the baby."

"You don't know that," he said, trying his best to be calm.

"No, it's over, it's over," I kept repeating, refusing to be filled with false hope.

He called the doctor's after-hours line, and the nurse told us to come in the following morning. I fell asleep that night out of sheer exhaustion. At 6:45 a.m., we were back at the doctor's office. I held my breath as the tech began searching for the baby. Without saying a word, she turned up the volume—and there it was: a healthy heartbeat. I collapsed into the ugliest, most violent sobbing, the kind where I had to be told to breathe so I wouldn't hyperventilate.

"What was all the blood from, then?" I asked.

It could've been from the progesterone suppositories, the doctor suggested. I was told to expect a bit more blood and to stay off my feet as much as possible. The bleeding continued lightly off and on for the next few days and then tapered off.

But fifteen days later, the bleeding started again. It was heavier, more aggressive, and more ominous. I panicked. I didn't want to tell my husband. I didn't want it to be real. I was losing my baby this time, I just knew it—and it was all my fault. My husband found me naked and hysterical on the bathroom floor, rocking back and forth, grieving the loss of the little person I was convinced I'd never know. I was soaking maxi pads with blood; it was the telltale sign that a miscarriage was inevitable. The guilt swallowed me whole. *After all, this was my fault. I did this to my baby—to us.*

The next morning, I drove to the doctor's office alone, readying myself for the bad news. We didn't have anyone to watch our daughter, and part of me wanted to do this on my own. I don't know why; it feels so dumb now. But pregnancy really is a one-(wo)man job, no matter how many people are around you.

Just as he did last time, the doctor looked for the baby—and there was a perfect heartbeat. This time, the doctor spent a bit more time looking around for the culprit of this bleeding but couldn't find anything abnormal. My strong little baby had survived yet again, but I couldn't feel quite as relieved. "There was so much blood," I said. "It doesn't make sense."

He put me on modified bed rest and told me not to overanalyze it. I'm sure he was just trying to reduce my stress, but how could I not overanalyze it? I knew something was wrong. I stopped talking baby names with my husband, stopped Pinterest-boarding nurseries, stopped planning for the baby altogether.

A week later, the bleeding began again. Coincidentally, I had an appointment with my obstetrician that afternoon. I sat in the waiting room for over an hour surrounded by women with beautiful round bellies and continued to bleed. My husband kept asking the receptionist how much longer, but it wasn't until my sobs started to attract the attention of other patients that a nurse ushered me into an ultrasound room.

Up until then, all of my ultrasounds had been vaginal, but the tech said I was far enough along for an abdominal ultrasound. It took her about fifteen seconds to find the subchorionic hematoma (SCH)—basically, a giant blood-filled bruise—that was resting alongside my baby. Before that moment, I'd never heard of SCHs. I learned mine was on the larger side, and bigger wasn't better. If the SCH continued to grow, it could cause preterm labor and basically push the baby out.

My husband and I didn't know what to say. On one hand, we were relieved that there was an actual source of the bleeding, but now we were terrified for all new reasons.

"Could this have been caused by the HSG?" I asked.

She shrugged. "There's really no way of knowing." (SCHs are usually caused when the embryo detaches from the uterine wall and reattaches, which is likely what happened during the HSG.)

We stared at the ultrasound monitor of our baby and the big black monster floating next to it.

"Do you know the sex?" asked the ultrasound tech.

"Not yet," I said.

"Do you want to know?" she asked.

We looked at each other and nodded.

"Congratulations, you have a very strong little boy on your hands."

I sobbed. The baby we so desperately wanted was on the screen in front of me, and I wasn't sure if I'd ever get to hold him or kiss him.

From that point forward, I was on total bed rest. Not only was I to stay off my feet, I couldn't even sit upright at my desk, at the dinner table, or even in bed! I needed to be horizontal at all times. The hope was that with minimal activity, the baby would grow and the SCH would shrink before ultimately bleeding out or being reabsorbed.

Here's the thing about having more than one kid: the more children you have, the more opportunities there are to feel like you're completely blowing it.

I felt guilty because my actions could cause me to lose my child.

I felt guilty that I didn't ask to take a pregnancy test.

I felt guilty that I wasn't in tune enough with my body to know I was pregnant. (Even though I had a full meltdown days earlier because my husband had steamed up the bathroom, which caused all the curls to fall out of my hair. Hello, hormones!)

I felt guilty that my daughter might never know her brother.

I felt guilty that I might rob my husband of his son.

I felt guilty that I could no longer pick up my daughter.

I felt guilty that I couldn't watch Tallulah on my own because I couldn't leave bed.

I felt guilty because I let her watch way too many movies since it was the only thing we could do together. (She loved this part, though.)

I felt guilty putting everything on my husband's shoulders.

I felt guilty not driving her to school or making her dinners.

I felt guilty because it was over the holidays and I wanted so desperately to make the time special for her.

I felt guilty because I knew how much she wanted my attention, but I was so consumed with my pregnancy.

As you know if you're reading this book, my son survived. The SCH finally disappeared at around twenty weeks, and I was able to move on and feel guilty about new things. It was a long road but worth every moment because my family got the outcome we prayed for. The point of this isn't to explain our crazy pregnancy experience but rather to highlight the amount of responsibility I put on myself for something I couldn't have helped. Every step in the process was taken with the goal of one day having a happy, healthy baby, and I felt like my actions jeopardized that goal. I sat in so much guilt. I wallowed in it. I bathed in it. ALL OF THE GUILT.

I didn't need guilt; I needed a damn miracle . . . and I got one. His name is Roman.

As mamas, we allow ourselves to wear so much guilt because the pressures and expectations we put on ourselves is insane. For better or worse, we just have to get comfortable in it, because it's not going away. Not to get all psych major on you, but I think mamas need to acknowledge the feeling and move the fuck on.

Because here's the thing: I'm going to struggle with mom guilt every single day.

SHIT YOU NEED TO STOP FEELING GUILTY ABOUT.

Going to work out.

Having lunch with friends.

Missing bedtime.

Not generating a better income.

Leaving your baby with childcare when you're working.

Leaving your baby with childcare when you're not working.

Not having more patience.

Not having time to sanitize pump parts.

Not doing more tummy time.

Letting your baby cry during tummy time.

Going out on date night.

Drinking wine and having to dump your milk.

Drinking wine and *not* dumping your milk.

Giving your baby toys with batteries.

Quitting breastfeeding.

Skipping story time.

Letting your child watch TV or an iPad.

Breaking from your child's routine.

Being so strict about your child's routine.

Daydreaming about life before baby.

Spending money on yourself.

Picking your baby up late from nursery school or day care.

Reading a book that isn't about parenting.

Crying in front of your kid.

Giving your baby nonorganic, non-grain-free, non-homemade snacks.

Giving your baby organic, grain-free, homemade snacks (while you eat a cheeseburger).

Letting your baby cry at bedtime when you're sleep training.

Noticing your baby is overtired.

Not feeling guilty.

* * *

And mom guilt is in no way reserved for those "holy shit!" moments like during my pregnancy. It is rooted in our day-to-day routines: Do I make my kid a fresh smoothie for breakfast or do I shove a frozen waffle in the toaster? A fresh smoothie means giving her a healthier meal, but a waffle means I'll have a few more minutes to spend with her. What choice do I make? I'm losing something either way.

"Adult-ing" may be hard, but "mom-ing" can feel fucking impossible.

* * *

Mom guilt doesn't always manifest from a place of wanting to give wholly of ourselves to our child; in fact, sometimes our guilt comes from a place of wanting desperately to take a break from being a mom.

When Tallulah was just five months old, I was offered an amazing opportunity: one of my closest friends was developing a new lifestyle book and wanted me to work on it with her. The project itself would take about nine months, start to finish.

"Are you sure you're up for it?" she asked. Since Tallulah was still pretty small, she wanted to be respectful and make sure I was ready for such a big commitment.

"One hundred percent," I remember telling her.

Going back to work meant that I could regain a sense of self, even for just a few hours a day.

This project, however, wasn't going to be a typical collaboration. Beyond the time I'd spend soaking up the luminescent glow of my computer screen, this book would also require me to spend a lot of time on set. It was going to be photo-driven and highly visual, and, as the collaborator, I was going to be involved in most aspects of its creation.

We spent the first few months planning. We'd get together once a week and work on the structure of the book: vision boards and outlines and color stories and the deepest of deep dives on Pinterest. It was a nice departure from home life without the full-time commitment yet; a slow reentry into the land of the living.

However, as spring turned to summer, the project went into full swing. From the first week in July through the end of September, I was basically a ship passing my husband in the night. Summer came and went in a ferocious blur. I was creating and producing. I was opinionated, I was powerful. I was something other than a mother. I was my own woman. And the more I began to feel like myself again, the deeper my appreciation grew for the other part of my world.

Back at home, Tallulah learned to crawl that summer. She dropped a nap and started playing with toys. She was transitioning from baby to toddler . . . and I was missing it.

On one of our final shoot days, my husband was planning to take Tallulah to her very first birthday party. That morning, I laid out a sleeveless blue pinstripe dress with a red flower, her white sandals, and a red bow for her hair, and then I went to work.

I asked my husband to swing by the set after her party since they would be in the area. Being a proud mama, I wanted my colleagues to meet the rambunctious little girl they had heard me talk about all summer.

When he arrived, I rushed out to the car. My husband rolled down the window, beaming with pride and putting his finger to his lips.

"Shhh!" he said. "She had so much fun . . . she totally crashed out. I couldn't keep her up!"

I didn't believe it; our daughter never slept in the car. She never slept anywhere that wasn't her room. She was not the sleep-anywhere kind of baby (as established in Chapter 11). Quietly, I opened the back door and looked at my baby—who didn't look that much like a baby anymore—sound asleep after attending her first party. I couldn't help but think that she had grown since that morning. She was almost a toddler now, a big kid! And big kids pass out in the car after birthday parties and too much cake. She looked precious, and happy, and I couldn't help but think that my little girl would never know that I got to see her in her very first party dress.

I closed the door and thanked him for coming by but agreed it was best to let her sleep. In that moment, I felt so overwhelmingly empty. I had missed out on something that felt so silly but also so outrageously important. I had missed a moment. The guilt washed over me like a tidal wave.

I missed my daughter's first summer. I missed her first crawl. I missed taking her to her very first birthday party. I had missed a lot of firsts, and for a moment, I couldn't breathe.

Had I chosen myself over my baby? Had I been selfish? Did I make the wrong decision and squander this beautiful time I would never get back? Or was I a better mom for being away? Would I have resented it if I spent the summer at home, knowing that I passed on an opportunity to create something amazing?

Honestly, I don't know the answers. But I am pretty certain that I was bound to feel like shit either way. That's how this mom guilt thing works. What I do know is that it was a really incredible project, and though I'm beyond grateful to have had the opportunity, I'm still going to grieve the moments I lost. I think that's normal.

Going back to work allowed me to reclaim a part of who I was, and through that experience, I realized that I also had this new, intrinsic part of my identity: my daughter. I could never fully disconnect from her, because she was as much a part of me as anything. She was woven into the very fabric of my identity; the most important part of me . . . but not the only part. And in finding that balance is where we also find the guilt.

Whether you're a working mom or a stay-at-home mom, it doesn't really matter, because the bottom line is this: you're not always going to be able to be there when you want to be or when your child wants you to be. No choice is the perfect choice because everything comes with a flip side. No matter what you do, no matter how well you can balance, and no matter how many hours of sleep you skip trying to be everything to everyone, at some point you're going to break some dishes. No mom is perfect, and no child expects you to be.

As mamas, we just need to start embracing the idea that we're going to let ourselves down sometimes and that it's okay.

Even if I one day discover how to "have it all" and "do it all," I don't think the guilt will go away when I'm not able to do and be everything for my kids. And until I can figure out how to clone myself, I'm just going to have to get used to feeling a bit guilty.

Your little person just needs you to do your best and to love them unconditionally. If you're there to kiss their knee when they fall down, that's amazing. But if you're there during nighttime cuddles to listen to them tell you the story of their fall, that's pretty great too. You don't need to make gourmet baby food for them to know you love them. You're allowed to turn on the TV to occupy them when you've had a hard day, and you can let them eat the icing out of the bowl. Your baby will survive if he or she plays with battery-operated toys and if she cries for a bit during tummy time or before nap time. Your baby won't go to therapy because he or she was the last one picked up from nursery school a couple times or because you went to lunch with your friends. Most of all, your baby will never resent you for doing your absolute best when trying to balance all the pieces of your life.

I've learned to live with my mom guilt. I recognize that it's just a feeling and that my inability to be all things to all people isn't going to permanently damage my child.

Mamas, we need to embrace our mom guilt because it is a beautiful reminder of how much we love our children, how everything we do in some shape or form is for our children. It is also a reminder of how much we deserve a glass of wine at the end of the day—and that is one thing we definitely should *not* feel guilty about!

A SELFISH MOM IS AN AWESOME MOM

16

"This was such a dumb idea!" I bemoaned over the Bluetooth speaker, racing to my coffee date, irritated for missing my own deadline.

I'm not exactly sure why I thought I could manage writing a book, caring for a preschooler, and keeping a newborn alive at the same time—but the heavens aligned and they were meant to coexist during the same foggy summer for a reason. Experiencing all the turmoil of Roman's infancy as I wrote this book helped me tap into all those forgotten emotions of Tallulah's first days. When parents tell you that they "can't remember" what it was like to bring a newborn home, it's not an exaggeration.

I call it postpartum amnesia, or maybe it's just Darwin's theory of survival of the fittest; either way, for many of us, it's a necessary stage if we are ever to procreate again. But let me tell you, when the next child is born, it comes rolling back like a thunderstorm.

For those of you wondering: no, having a second child is not as insane as the first, at least not for me. Tallulah already had a firm grip on my world, so when we brought Roman home, my life was already complete pandemonium. He was just another log on the fire. (But I'll save all that for another book. If nothing else, my having another child should give you all great comfort. I mean, if I decided to do it again after everything I went through with the first one, there is hope for every one of you.)

Throughout this book, I've talked a lot about the importance of self-care, but no matter how often or how loudly I shout it from the rooftops, I still don't believe that's enough. No matter how many times I tell a new mom that she needs to nourish her own person in order to be a good mom, she will find some excuse to blow it off—I know this, because I'm often my own worst enemy.

A new mother, whether out of guilt or anxiety (or a combination of the two), will almost always sideline her needs first. And that, my friends, is a slippery fucking slope.

DUMB REASONS WE BLOW OFF SELF-CARE

I can't leave the baby for that long.

He's not taking a bottle that well yet.

I don't want to have to pump in the car.

I'm too tired.

If I go out, I might get sick. And if I get sick, he'll get sick. . . .

She's been really fussy this week; maybe next week.

He sleeps better if I'm holding him.

I really should finish reorganizing the kitchen.

I think I might be depressed.

I'm tired, depressed, and I haven't shaved my legs in a month.

But who will make dinner?

She's just really sensitive to my smell.

I can't afford it; babies are expensive.

I don't want anyone to see me looking like this.

I would, but he's going through a total "stranger danger" phase.

There's SO much laundry to do.

We're cutting a tooth, but next week for sure.

I know I'll miss these moments later. . . .

* * *

Between work and the constant demands of mom life, finding any me time was nearly impossible. While I attempted to write this very chapter, my husband suggested I schedule a coffee date with two of my girlfriends.

A coffee date! Do you know the last time I interacted with other adults in some place other than a doctor's office? Do you know the last time I went somewhere alone that wasn't the grocery store or CVS on a late-night infant Tylenol run? (Teething is a real bitch.) That's about as glamorous as it gets, ladies.

Before you give my husband more credit than he deserves, I firmly believe that this was his attempt at self-preservation. He went out of his way to make sure I got a little me time so he wouldn't have to buy a new iPhone. After all, if I tossed his out another window, he would certainly not be as lucky as the first time.

That being said, it did mean he was listening—which is progress! A few weeks earlier, my girlfriends asked me to join them for lunch at a hip new restaurant. Unfortunately, it was about thirty minutes away and I had to tell them that I wasn't ready to venture that far yet with the little guy. What if he got hungry on the road? My nerves were pretty delicate, and it was best to keep things predictable. The last thing I needed was to get a parking ticket for stopping to nurse my baby in a passenger loading zone. (Yes, that really has happened.) I expected my friends to suggest a closer restaurant for us . . . but they didn't. They went without me, and I was irrationally heartbroken.

So, when my husband offered to leave work early so I could go meet my friends, I gladly accepted but told him I was going to schedule it for the end of the week (knowing that I wouldn't enjoy it unless I got some work done and was able to pump enough to have a few bottles on tap for Roman while I was gone). I told myself that it was a special treat for making it through another week with two kids, and for finally making some progress with work.

Monday became Tuesday, which turned into Wednesday and Thursday . . . and I hadn't done shit. My days went by in a haze of constant breastfeeding and doctor appointments and preschool drop-offs, and I made *zero* headway on this chapter. Even when I managed to sneak into my office for an hour or two, I couldn't find the words. I just stared at the blank computer screen until something pulled my attention away (usually the Target app or Amazon Prime).

When Friday arrived, I felt totally defeated. What had I even done all week? Whatever it was, it definitely was not deserving of any self-care, so I started making excuses as to why I needed to call and cancel (please see the sidebar on page 224). My husband gave me a very stern look, which I took to mean, "Oh, no, bitch, I didn't leave work just to sit here and watch you mope."

I pulled on my new jean shorts—a pair I had begrudgingly ordered two sizes larger than my normal waistline, because . . . mom bod—and tied my hair into a ratty topknot using my daughter's rainbow-colored scrunchie. On my way there, I called my husband to lament my decision in hopes that he would take pity on me and tell me that I could turn around.

"This is a huge waste of time," I spouted over the Bluetooth. "I should be writing, or pumping. I should be spending time with Tallulah. I don't feel like I get any time with her."

"Leslie, stop," he said. "Quit trying to find a reason to beat yourself up. Have fun."

Click.

I was looking for a pep talk; he clearly didn't have the patience for it. I started crying and told myself that this is why we don't buy our daughter presents before she earns them. I hadn't earned this coffee date. And my daughter currently has a brand-new bicycle that she was only supposed to get once she started staying in her bed all night; yet I routinely find her on the couch at three in the morning singing "Rudolph the Red-Nosed Reindeer" in Spanish. (Don't ask.)

When I got to the coffee shop, I sat in the parking lot for a few minutes trying to salvage my general appearance with a bit of lip balm and a nail file, and that's when I heard it. . . .

"Leslie?" said a woman with a familiar face, tapping on the driver's side window of my car.

"Hey, Mo!" I mustered, stepping out of the car and pulling her into a hug. I had known Maureen for over fifteen years but hadn't seen her since before I had my daughter.

"What are you up to?" she asked.

"I'm meeting some friends for coffee . . ." I started, pointing at the pink café about twenty yards away.

"Good for you!" she exclaimed, with the sort of fist-pumping encouragement you would expect someone to give a new mom. In the age of social media, almost everyone in our universe is kept abreast of major milestones, and Mo knew that I recently had had a baby.

That's when I unloaded: "I don't know. I feel so dumb. My boobs are about to explode and I'm exhausted . . . and don't even look at my hair! I have so much work to do today and this just feels like I'm being selfish. I was upset over this lunch date, and it is so immature. I don't really have this kind of time right now."

I don't know what I expected her to say, but I couldn't help the word-vomit; I just needed someone to feel sorry for me.

"Yes, you do," she said simply and matter-of-factly.

"No, you don't understand, I'm writing this book and . . ." I continued.

"Yes, you do," she said again, more firmly but with a smile on her face. "You're already standing here. You have the time."

"But if I'm not working, I really need to be at home with . . ."

"Leslie," she interrupted and grabbed me by both shoulders. "I read all the shit you put on Instagram and watch the videos you post. You just had a baby, and you need to make time to care for yourself. If you were me, what would you tell you right now?"

She paused as I thought about that for a moment.

"Honey, you need to take your own medicine."

Well, shit. That is what you call getting served some truth salad.

I'm not a super spiritual person, but I definitely believe the parenting gods were shining on me in that moment. I knew that the best thing I could do for myself and my family was to enjoy the shit out of my coffee date. If I spent the next hour getting in my own head and making lists of all the shit I still had to do or feeling guilty for being away, I would go back home feeling anxious and stressed.

But, if I actually allowed myself to relax and embrace this time to catch up with my friends, I might leave a better mother, wife, and overall human.

And I did. Not only did I get to spend time with some of my favorite people, but I also drank an entire iced latte before it got watered down. I left the ninety-minute coffee date feeling calmer, more balanced, and better equipped to tackle the rest of my day.

Okay, so I know I spent the last few pages bitching about being forced to meet my friends for coffee. For most new moms, that sounds like a damn spa weekend! If I were reading this, I'd want to slap me, but whether or not I'm annoying isn't the point. (For the record, I know I am.) The point is that, as a new mom, I needed a fucking break, and giving myself that break ended up doing more for my family and myself than if I had just sat at home feeling miserable and depleted.

There's only so long you can burn the candle at both ends before you end up sitting in the dark. To have a healthy postpartum experience, it is necessary for all mothers, especially new ones, to take meaningful moments to indulge in the type of self-care that actually fills their cup.

To be clear, this does not include leaving your baby for ten minutes to pick up the dry cleaning or handing over baby duties to someone else while you pump. The prerequisite is that whatever you choose to do must be completely for yourself; this is your time to reclaim something that makes you happy, whether it's three minutes or thirty.

Look, I'm not saying you should pack a bag and head out on a six-week European vacation; but if you're depriving yourself of a baby-free trip to the mall, then you really need to pull your head out of the sand (I say that with love). Do something that you used to enjoy prior to having a baby: journal, find a new hiking trail, go for a drive and listen to a podcast, get your eyebrows waxed . . . whatever!

In this new culture of the unicorn mom, we wear our sacrifice as a badge of honor, but I don't find it all that honorable. Why do we feel the need to compete over who is more exhausted? It's like the less we do for ourselves somehow equates to us being better moms. Motherhood certainly comes with enormous sacrifice, but our sense of self-worth and mental stability is not intended to be one of them (despite how it might feel sometimes).

When and how did martyrdom become the universal symbol of good parenting? I think being a martyr for your child and your family is way more self-serving than taking time for self-care. Failing to nurture ourselves can harm our postpartum experience. Think about it: How can we expect to be great moms when we're feeling like garbage humans?

My postpartum journey was different with my second child because I was fully back to work—albeit working from home—by the time he was six weeks old and I had in-home childcare that allowed me the opportunity to leave the house on occasion for a meeting or an errand. For many new moms—working or stay-at-home—they spend those first three months at home alone with their newborn, and escaping isn't necessarily easy.

Strike that. Let me rephrase: asking for help isn't necessarily easy.

Unless you live on lonely island, I pretty much guarantee there is a friend, family member, or neighbor you could trust to properly care for your child for a short window of time. It might not be the most ideal situation, it might put your postpartum anxiety on high alert, and you might come home to your mother-in-law Facetiming Iran with your newborn (or maybe that's just me), but what's the real harm? And taking fifteen minutes to go for a walk might be the difference of having a good day or having a breakdown.

Let me warn you that perhaps your mothers and grandmothers will opine about how they never quite felt the urge to break free, but remember how different this generation of women is from any other. We were bred and groomed to have stronger senses of self and identity and therefore our needs as mothers will *of course* be different.

I believe that the identity loss we experience as women during the postpartum period is crippling our overall motherhood experience. It's impossible to be a good anything when we're struggling to figure out who the hell we are in these new roles—and the longer it takes for new moms to acclimate, the more challenging it becomes. Like anything, the larger you allow the problem to grow, the harder it is to overcome.

As counterintuitive as it might seem, being the best mom I could be meant that I needed to do things to reclaim pieces of my non-mom identity.

I knew who I was prior to becoming "mama," but I also knew I wasn't her anymore. And therein lies the rub. Once that baby is born, there is no time machine. Even if I ever happen to find myself kid-free and in Las Vegas for the night, I can only wear heels for about forty-five minutes and will likely be asleep before *Saturday Night Live* starts . . . on East Coast time.

The things I value have forever shifted. How I enjoy my time has forever shifted. Am I totally fulfilled by the day-to-day grind of motherhood? No. But do I feel a pang of sadness if I'm away from my kids for too long? Yes. And that's okay. Actually, that's more than okay, that should be *expected*. I am allowed to be my own woman and a mom. I can wear both hats.

Understanding our new roles doesn't happen overnight; like all motherhood, it's a journey and often a messy one. Which is why it's *essential* that we take the time to get to know our new selves, starting in those very early days when we feel the most disconnected. How you go about procuring this new self-realization is entirely personal (yet another thing to put on your to-do list!).

Did you love to cook prior to having a baby? Great! Figure out how cooking works into your new life. Are you a bookworm? Me too. Make it a point to find twenty minutes a day to read. I do it in the evenings after bedtime, but maybe for you it works better early in the morning or during nap time. It's trial and error. For the record, it's a hell of a lot easier to accomplish if you put down the damn phone too (trust me, I'm just as guilty of this). Decide which parts of your pre-parent identity give you the most fulfillment and make the effort to incorporate them into your new life.

No checklist I can offer you will be as important as figuring out for yourself what gives you joy, release, and respite.

It's so easy to get in these ruts of self-pity. So, remind yourself that taking care of YOU is important not just for your own peace of mind but also for everyone in your family. Yes, it might be a pain in the ass to prep your husband for two hours just so you can leave the house for forty-five minutes, and it might feel overwhelming to leave your newborn with a friend who doesn't have the baby's cries memorized. But remind yourself that your baby will survive, and everyone will be better for it.

You can only be the best daughter, wife, friend, and mom when you're being the best YOU. And don't your kids deserve the best? Being a little more selfish might just be the most selfless thing you can do.

17

MOTHERHOOD DOESN'T COME WITH AN EPIDURAL

In writing this book, I've sometimes wondered—feared, really—if people are going to read it and think I'm a bad mom or that I don't adore my children as much as I really do.

I can see where they'd be coming from. My transition into motherhood was a total shit show, and no one handed me an operator's manual. My life, my world was completely turned upside down when my daughter was born, and piecing together our new life as a family wasn't easy, or pretty. I wasn't prepared for my new role, and I didn't always make the best choices or decisions—and it would appear that I had a tendency to lose my temper.

Becoming a mom uncovered some of my deepest insecurities, while forcing me to desert the life I had spent three decades creating. All of the armor I built up over the years was savaged by a beautiful, destructive little human who brought me to my unshowered, unshaven knees. I had to grieve that loss and then move the fuck on for the sake of my new family. It's not fair what modern women go through in making this voyage, without many of the resources we as mothers so desperately need, but I also think that we're warriors because we do it. We realize it's for our children and we suit up to play.

You're going to sacrifice because motherhood is an incredible sacrifice. Being a mother and having a family are blessings and tremendous privileges. Most days and in most instances, you're going to prioritize the needs of your family over your own, which isn't always convenient, but we do it anyway.

I'm usually happy to make the sacrifice, whether it's a dinner date, a workout class, more time behind my computer, or a clean house. I also choose to relinquish every one of my weekends to kids' birthday parties and soccer camps. I love my family endlessly and I'll do whatever I need to if I believe it is in their best interest, but sometimes it's really fucking hard. Sometimes those sacrifices aren't little things that you can brush off with ease; sometimes they're monumental. Sometimes, they'll change the course of your life.

When Tallulah was eighteen months old, my husband and I decided that it was time to move. After six and a half years in our little Hollywood bungalow, we were bursting at the seams.

I've never been overly emotional when it comes to moving, and I've moved quite a bit over the years. I've never once attempted to re-create the final scene of a sitcom when the main character stands in the doorway and, before walking out, glances back over her shoulder for one last look at the now empty room.

But this time, it was different. Aside from the actual logistics of packing up our lives and uncovering what had been living at the bottom of our "garage freezer" for the past half decade, leaving the house was emotionally taxing. This house was special. I had lived in this home longer than any other place since I was twelve years old. My husband and I moved into this place as newlyweds; it was where we started our life together. We learned so much about who we were within these walls. It was where we built our careers and our marriage. It was where my husband brought home my beloved Archie—a rescue doodle with serious anxiety and cat-like tendencies—as a thirtieth birthday present for me. It was within these walls that my husband and I received bad news and had tough conversations. It was where we laughed, loved, and built the foundation of our little world.

It was also within these walls where we celebrated. It was where we planned, prepped, and panicked for the arrival of our first child. It was where my husband illegally painted our front curb red so my pregnant butt could waddle in and out of our front gate with ease. It was where we brought Tallulah home for the first time. It was where we spent so many sleepless nights, and where we argued over whose turn it was to warm up the milk. It was where she smiled for the first time, and where she took her first steps. It was where my husband and I learned what it meant to be parents, and a family.

It broke my heart to think about saying goodbye because I always thought we'd be in this house forever, but I was comforted by the promise of our new home and new memories to be made. When we started looking at homes around LA that would accommodate the needs of our family and ones in "great school districts," we realized that every house in our budget came with a sacrifice: no backyard, small bedrooms, less-than-stellar schools, busy streets, no nearby parks, and so forth. If we decided to push out into more affordable neighborhoods, it meant a longer commute for my husband and less time he'd be able to be home with Tallulah; the time with her was already so fleeting.

That's when he proposed the idea of moving back to my hometown. We had toyed with the idea of going back to Orange County, but never in the immediate future. He made the argument that my parents would be nearby, that he could easily move his business to the area, and that the schools were great and the homes more affordable. It made sense on paper.

At first glance, moving back to a familiar place with built-in support might seem to make for a smooth transition, but, trust me, I love nothing more than making seemingly simple things difficult, overanalyzed, and entirely too complex.

I loved living in Los Angeles, and I never thought I'd leave. Moving to Orange County was the best decision for all of us and I agreed to it, but it was still hard to pull the trigger.

Look, I totally get that I'm bitching about having to move back to Laguna Beach, which in the category of hometowns is pretty up there. But without getting too much into the twisted web that is my own psychology, moving back meant that I was being forced to abandon the place where I had set roots for the last near decade, a town that was an enormous part of who I was.

And that really was the rub. Moving away felt like I was forfeiting the last piece of my pre-baby identity. Perhaps I held on to the city because it gave me an iota of street cred ("I may drive a soccer mom mobile and I may have Puffs littering the backseat, but at least I live in LA"). Heading to the suburbs would mean that my total mom life transition would be complete.

In part, moving back home represented my coming full circle and closing the loop on a really huge part of my life. Looking back on the past fourteen years and thinking about who I am today versus who I was when I left, I realize that I'm not the same person as I was in 2004. I watch *Dateline* on Friday nights. I wash my hair three times a week max, and I go months without putting on a pair of high heels. The last time I went to a nightclub, I shouted to the server—over music blaring at a preposterous decibel—to bring me a glass of "white wine" and he came back ready to hand me a napkin full of "wide limes." He then apologized and called me "ma'am." I yell at kids who are roughhousing in the hotel pool, and I wear too much SPF. I don't spend money on clothes for myself or my husband; instead, I have an Amazon Subscribe and Save account that keeps me fully stocked on paper towels, laundry pods, and alkaline water (because you can't put a price tag on proper hydration). I'd rather spend time braiding my daughter's hair and snuggling with her on the couch than flipping through the latest *Travel & Leisure* (where the hell am I going to go, anyway?), and I can't tell you the last time I went to a bottomless mimosa brunch.

Throughout this book, I've bloviated about how a mother's happiness equates with the overall happiness of the family, and I stand by that statement. But what makes me truly happy now is no longer the same as it was before I had my daughter.

Seeing her jump up and down on the trampoline in the backyard makes me happy, and so does watching her make new friends on the seesaw at the neighborhood park. Sitting at the kitchen counter making cookies together and being there to wipe away her tears when she tells me a friend at school didn't want to play. Watching her grow into the world around her and giving her everything I can and being the best version of myself for her—that's what makes me happy.

And it doesn't matter what zip code I do this in as long as I am with my family.

A mother's self-care is the bedrock for a happy family dynamic. But as mothers, the axis of our world has shifted. We can find happiness in ourselves and in the children we created. Certainly, I still crave a night out with girlfriends, and I never feel so put together as when I have time to pluck my eyebrows, but those are the moments we squeeze in to nurture our own person and recharge our batteries.

None of this came to me overnight. It was a long, winding road from the hospital to here, and I still miss parts of my life and my freedom that I had before starting a family—and I expect all of you to, as well! Being a mom doesn't mean I can't miss outdoor concerts, afternoons spent window shopping, and taking quiet car rides. It doesn't mean I can't miss certain friends whose calls come further and further apart. (Or texts, because no one calls me on the phone. I don't associate with psychopaths.) It doesn't mean I can't miss lazy Sundays at the pool and staying till the end of the Super Bowl Party because I'm not worried about bedtimes.

But for so long after having Tallulah, I focused on what I was giving up in motherhood and not enough on what I was gaining. Saying goodbye is an important part of the process and one I wish I would have known about before giving birth, but I also never knew how fulfilling it could be either. Women who become mothers are so busy running around like chickens with their heads cut off that they never stop and tell new moms, "My life is chaos and I drink more wine than I probably should, but I love my family so much it takes my fucking breath away."

It's complicated and difficult to manage; we are required to wear so many hats and have all the answers before we even fully understand the question. We're asked to give all of ourselves at any time, and we're forced to drop everything in front of us if we get a call saying "she has a fever" or "he had a fall." We become the lowest-ranking member of our own army, but somehow hold the most responsibility.

There are no one-size-fits-all answers when it comes to motherhood. You're going to do what you think is best, and I'm going to do the same. I'm not going to tell you it gets easier or one day you'll stop worrying, because it doesn't and you won't. You know what they say: little kids, little problems; big kids, fucking gargantuan problems. (They say that, right?) But one day you'll wake up and realize you don't mind the challenge or the worry, because what's the alternative?

I can't tell you that you're going to love your life every single moment or that all of the chaos of your world will magically fall into place. What I can tell you is that you just read a book about trying to be the best mom you can be, so I'm pretty sure you love the shit out of your kid, just like I love mine. I love them so much it hurts, and I would go through it all ten times over for ten times as long if in the end I would still get my wickedly funny, insanely smart Tallulah, temper tantrums and all, and Roman, my peaceful little warrior,

"I'll never be the type of mom who just parks my kids in front of the TV. If we go to a restaurant, they'll know to behave."

Oh yes, that's right. I was that asshole. I sat there—childless, showered, and picking at a salmon salad—completely oblivious to what this woman's day had been like and what it took to get herself to that restaurant. Yet, somehow, I felt like I had the license to make nasty comments because I'd seen enough shared articles on Facebook to believe myself an expert on the "screen time" debate, even though I had no child of my own yet and my wealth of knowledge came from the internet. What right did I have to consider her a "lesser" parent because she let her kids watch television during lunch? The fact is, I didn't. I didn't know anything about anything when it came to being a mother, and even that is an understatement.

Much like breastfeeding and coconut LaCroix, television is the subject of rigorous debate in our modern mama culture. My parents grew up without a TV, so when I was born they figured it was just one of the many modern perks of having kids in the eighties (along with Cabbage Patch Kids, *Fraggle Rock,* and Super Mario Bros. 3). By all accounts, television was a luxury and not the monster that it's become today. However, by 2013—after a rather large backlash to Disney's Baby Einstein courtesy of a Federal Trade Commission filing circa 2006—television, and screen time in general, was largely considered detrimental to early childhood development. And like most things pertaining to parenthood, once television was anointed the devil, people everywhere felt they had an obligation to criticize parents who were still allowing their child to enjoy screen time.

That woman in the restaurant didn't deserve my judgment; she deserved a damn parade for getting a set of toddler twins into a restaurant. I get that now. She just needed a break, and an episode of *Paw Patrol* or *Daniel Tiger's Neighborhood* was just what the doctor ordered. After a long day, I might just want to cook dinner and watch the news in peace, and if that means my daughter is going to sit her little butt in front of the iPad for twenty-seven minutes, that's okay.

whose smile reduces me to tears. There is nothing on this planet that I wouldn't do for them, and if anything, my journey has forced me to work my ass off every single day to be the best mother I can be.

I decided to write this book after surviving that first year as a new mom and after finally realizing that all the doubt and guilt and confusion I felt was normal. I know one day she'll read this and say, "Gee, Mom, thanks," but my struggles in becoming a mother weren't about her (I mean, they were, but they weren't); they were about me.

I've discovered new parts of my identity, shed pieces of me that no longer fit, and fought to hold on to the things I value most. It's a dance, and often it's not very graceful, but you'll get the hang of it.

I usually get so stressed out with all the things I think I should be doing as a mom that I forget to remind myself that just being here is sometimes enough. We weigh ourselves down with the accessories of motherhood and forget to give ourselves credit for the commitment we make to motherhood, day in and day out.

Our children don't need us to be perfect, they need us to be happy, healthy, and present.

They don't necessarily need organic flaxseed muffins or Pinterest-worthy creative play activities. They just need us.

They will survive if some days we forget to brush their hair as we run out the door or hurry through the bedtime routine because our day has eaten us alive.

They don't need us to slay it, crush it, kill it, or nail it.

They need our attention and our love and the stability of our presence. And even when we're messy, imperfect, unfiltered, and unshowered . . . they just need us.

Unlike labor, motherhood doesn't come with an epidural. You're not going to do everything right as a mom. You're going to lose your temper and your mind. You're going to cry the first time you realize you can't feed her the way you want and when you have to hand him off to someone else for safekeeping. You're going to be tired, very, very tired. You're going to have to say goodbye to certain people who can't relate to your new priorities, and for the first time in a long time, you'll be forced to make new friends (socializing . . . blech). You're going to need to appreciate and accept the skin you're in, which means loving that your hips are a bit wider and the crow's feet that you never noticed before that now crinkle the sides of your eyes. You're going to start saying things like "we don't drink bath water," "someone's having big feelings today," and "how much sodium does it have?"

Becoming a mother will test you and push you and fill a part of your soul that you never knew existed. It will teach you how strong you are, how your body, no matter how ravaged, is a temple to be worshipped. As a mother, you stand at the gateway of life and death and bring a human into this world. It's fucking insane, and incredible. You'll watch your child grow and see glimpses of yourself, your parents, your siblings, and your partner in her facial expressions or his movements. It's a miracle before your eyes. You'll realize that motherhood has given you an unimaginable grit; you would fight a pack of wolves for your kid—and you would win. You are unbreakable, even in the moments you are sure you're cracking. Being a mother makes you a damn superhero, and there is at least one set of eyes that will look at you like you can lift the world on your shoulders, because for him or her, you do.

And even though it rocked me to my core, I fucking love being a mom.

ACKNOWLEDGMENTS

A huge thank-you to the three most important men in my life who have had the displeasure of dealing with me throughout the creation of this book (and well, well beforehand): my husband, my father, and my agent.

To my husband, Yashaar, you get me and you love me anyway. You believed in me and in this project even when I started to lose faith. You're a fucking awesome dad, my best friend, my safe haven, and the second funniest person in this marriage. You stuck by me through every questionable hair choice I made, and that really says something about a person's character. Please dry off your feet after taking a shower.

To my dad, Robert, every little girl thinks her father is the best, but there is only one Bob Bruce in this world, and I'm forever lucky that you're mine. You've always been my biggest cheerleader; you're the most decent and most honorable man I've ever known. Everything I've ever done right is because of you, but don't call me three times in a row. That's fucking psycho. I'll never answer. (Also, sorry I swear so much.)

To my agent, Matthew Elblonk, you pulled a rabbit out of a hat. I can't properly express how grateful I am; you made the biggest dream of my life come true, and I am forever indebted to you. Thank you for being my champion, my voice of reason, my strongest ally, and, most importantly, my friend. I'm beyond grateful that your parents got buzzed at that Fourth of July bicentennial in '76. I promise I won't make you listen to any more stories about breastfeeding.

Thank you to my incredible mother, Sandra Bruce; I get it now and I can never repay you. You sacrificed so much so I could achieve my goals. This book is as much your accomplishment, as it is mine. Thank you for sitting with me during lunch in eighth grade. I'm sorry about the beer cap you found under the couch in 1999. I can tell you now . . . it was mine.

A huge thank-you to my editor, Laura Mazer. I could not have possibly imagined a more incredible partner on this journey. Your thoughtful guidance, your relatable wisdom, your patient support—this is a far better book for having you as part of its creation. You understood this project from the very start, and your involvement will directly benefit the women who read it. Thank you for taking a chance on me. I know I was a psycho about the subtitle, and I'm sorry.

Thank you to the entire team at Hachette: Chin-Yee Lai (a cover design wizard!), Michael Clark (a project editor who made this process manageable and kept us on track), Christina Palaia (the most thoughtful and diligent copy editor imaginable), Linda Mark (the magician who made my word document into an actual book), Sharon Kunz (the publicity genius who understood this book from the very start), and everyone who helped me on this journey. It was a pleasure working with each and every one of you; I am beyond grateful for your commitment to making this the best possible book.

Thank you to Lauren Tell and Yoni Goldberg. You believed in me from the beginning. You gave of your efforts, your time, and your talents in helping bring this idea to life. Yoni, you are such an incredible artist, yet you remain so humble and generous. That's a remarkable gift. Lauren, you are one of the most selfless people I've ever known. You work hard, fight for what you believe in, and carry yourself with grace. Most of all, you're a really, really good friend. That said, neither of you should ever be left alone with a campfire and camera. Stay in your lane.

Thank you to my village: Olga Castro, Margot Reyes, and April Torregroza. It takes remarkable women to care for someone else's family as if it were their own. I cannot thank you enough for supporting us and loving us, even our overweight rescue dog, Sherman.

Thank you, thank you, thank you to my girl tribe: Krystal Whitney, Cassandra Bergsland, Lindsay Pomer, Lauren Schutte, Jenny Managhebi, Casey Leavitt, Sydney Gilbert, Jeannie Scharetg, Aili Nahas, Emma Feil, Erin Bozek, Molly Fathy, Julie Harris, Lauren Stubblefield, Nicole Neves, Hannah Skvarla, Annie Bonfeld, Ilana Saul, Rachel Rosenbloom, Piper Lewis, Julie Rossing, Kelly Zajfen, Pamelyn Rocco, Holly Madison, Shannon Hammer, Jeni Castro, Brandi Glanville, Jen Salute, Tracy Robbins, Kallyn Adler, Natalie Friedman, Carolyn Reed, Jesse DeSanti, Danielle Estrada, Heidi Cascardo, Nadine Courtney, and Hannah Buehring. There's a special place in heaven for women who lift up other women. I'm blessed to know each and every one of you. I am humbled and honored to have had your support on this project. Thank you for trusting me with your own motherhood stories; especially my best friend who peed on a pile of diapers in a parking garage. I promise I'll never call you out by name, Cassandra.

Thank you to all the mamas in my family: Sharon Calandra, Jacqueline Daniels, Maryam Nabavi, my late grandmother Irene Stahulak, and all my crazy-ass aunts on the South Side of Chicago. I am beyond blessed to have spent my life surrounded by such incredible, fierce, compassionate, don't-take-shit-from-anybody women. You're awesome moms, but you're all fit for straitjackets. I love you.

Thank you to my unbelievable Unpacified community. This book wouldn't have been possible without all the incredible women I met and connected with through social media and unpacified.com. Thank you for supporting my journey, and sharing your own.

Thank you to the incredible women who lent their advice, knowledge, and support to this book: Paige Bellenbaum, Catherine Birndorf, Melissa Brown, Kimberly Johnson, Katya Libin, Carly Snyder, Heidi Stevens, and Alli Webb.

Thank you to Chrissy Teigen and her summer 2018 Instagram Stories series: *Headband of the Day*. It got me through some really rough patches.

Last, but certainly not least, to Tallulah and Roman. I never knew how beautiful life could be until I met you. You stole my heart and my sanity. You are my greatest joys and the absolute two best things I've ever done. I'm not always going to be perfect and I'm not always going to get it right, but I'm always going to be there. I'm going to try my absolute best and I'm always going to love you, you little shits.

EMMA FEIL PHOTOGRAPHY

Leslie Bruce is a *New York Times* best-selling coauthor and award-winning entertainment journalist, but she absolutely hates writing her own bio. She created online parenting platform Unpacified to give an unfiltered voice to the Modern Mama and to connect and support women on their motherhood journey. Leslie lives in Laguna Beach, California, with her husband, Yashaar, and their children, Tallulah and Roman.

www.unpacified.com
IG @leslieannebruce